Key Truths and Applications for a Christ-Like Walk

A 15-Week Study for Growing Closer to the Lord

JENNIFER HERNANDEZ

WESTBOW·
PRESS
A DIVISION OF THOMAS NELSON
& ZONDERVAN

WestBow Press books may be ordered through booksellers or by contacting:

WestBow Press
A Division of Thomas Nelson & Zondervan
1663 Liberty Drive
Bloomington, IN 47403
www.westbowpress.com
1 (866) 928-1240

ISBN: 978-1-4908-7114-1 (sc)
ISBN: 978-1-4908-7115-8 (e)

Library of Congress Control Number: 2015904900

Print information available on the last page.

WestBow Press rev. date: 03/03/2015

Contents

This Study Guide is dedicated to those
who desire growth in the Lord; to those who want to seek him so they may discover him.
It is my hope that you will find a new relationship, perhaps a restored
relationship or find yourself just growing deeper in his truths and love.

Acknowledgments

First, I acknowledge that I can't do anything without the Lord Jesus Christ sustaining me every day. He is my Savior and Lord. He leads me each day. I may take wrong turns or stumble along the way, but he always picks me up, dusts me off and leads me once again. Thank you, Jesus, for your faithfulness and unending love. Thank you for giving me words to share.

Second, I acknowledge my husband, Allen. He is always patient with me. He has supported this idea of writing a study from the beginning as he supports me in all my endeavors. He cares for me and our children with his whole heart. He has an admirable "God's in control" attitude. Thank you and I love you.

Thirdly, I acknowledge my parents:

My mom – There isn't anyone in the world like a mom. She always has an open heart and is ready to listen. She went to my softball games growing up, countless band concerts and always drove my friends and me to youth group. Now she is a wonderful grandmother to my children, too. I couldn't ask for more. Thank you, Mom

My dad – Dads, like moms, although it may be in a different way, hold a special place in a child's life, even a grown child. My dad, taught me many lessons in life about doing the right thing, the definition of integrity and the Golden Rule. Though I knew a long time ago I wanted to write one day, it wasn't until he started writing a couple years ago that it brought it to the forefront of my mind. Thank you, Dad

Next, I want to acknowledge my first pastor, Pastor Sinclair and his family as well as my youth pastor, Pastor Dan. Because of their faithfulness to lead a church and because of the truth they taught on Sundays and Wednesdays, because of the time they invested in kids and adults alike, I heard truth and had the opportunity to respond to the Lord. Thank you, Pastor Sinclair and PD

Finally, I want to acknowledge my most recent former pastor, who was my pastor for ten years. Pastor Doug, his wife Julie, and their children. Because you are faithful to God, when my family and I came to church every Sunday and Wednesday we were fed. We were fed truths from his word. God shaped us and molded us under your leadership. My children began a foundation of knowing the Lord that they will continue to grow in and hold fast to because of your faithfulness. So much of who I am as a Christian is because of your teachings and God working through you over the past ten years. Thank you, Doug, Julie and family.

Introduction

Maybe you are not one to believe in Jesus Christ. But, your friend invited you to his/ her study group so you reluctantly went and now here you are in front of this study guide. Or maybe you were browsing the shelf at a local store and decided to give it a try on your own. *This book is for you.* Stick with it. May you learn, ask questions, reflect and move forward in the knowledge of Jesus.

Maybe you are a new believer and want to grow in the Lord. You're not really sure what living for Christ means or what you should do, but you know he is your Lord and Savior so you desire to learn more. *This book is for you.*

Maybe you are a believer, mature in your faith of twenty, thirty, forty years or more. I'm so happy you have known Christ for a number of years and have trusted him for your salvation. But, I know that with maturity in the Lord it's easy to become complacent, stagnant and in need of refreshment. *This book is for you.*

Finally, maybe you are one who is a believer but have been backsliding. You have walked away from your faith. You have fallen into sin and have ignored God's outstretched hand to bring you back home to him. He's still reaching. He is your hope. *This book is for you.*

This study guide is in two parts:

Part I:

The first six weeks of this study guide is to reflect on your own relationship with Christ. You might think that's not necessary, especially if you've been a Christian for a longer length of time. But let me assure you it is always good to reflect on and examine your relationship with Christ. Before we can jump into some key truths and applications for being refreshed and grow in the Lord we need to first look at ourselves in the mirror. It may not always be fun (though I hope you find the study enjoyable) and it may be a little convicting, but it's necessary and for your benefit. After all, to grow in Lord is the name of the game. So for the first six lessons we will discuss "the basics." We will discuss what it even means to have a relationship with Christ and how. We'll also look at faith, being sure of your salvation, being transformed and having a sure foundation by building your house on the Rock. This study is for everyone. So, I pray you grow and if you're in a place of needing refreshment from the Lord and perhaps a reconnection with him in order to grow deeper, don't glaze over Part I just because it's "the basics." There are truths to be learned and realized. We know that God's Word is always fresh and relevant.

Part II:

Once we have covered the first six weeks, the next nine weeks will be lessons on living out your faith and growing in a deeper relationship with him all the while being refreshed and steadfast in the Lord. We will study, explore and learn about topics such as servant hood, acceptance, patience, stillness, God's omniscience, leaning on him, his unending love and more. I pray you enjoy and grow in Lord!

Each week has a place at the end of the week's lesson for you to record prayer requests for the week as well as praise reports and things in which you are thankful. If you are completing this study guide in a group setting it is suggested you review these in your group each week. Share the prayer requests as you are comfortable in order to be praying for one another. Share the praises and thanksgiving to glorify God and bring honor to him.

Please note that the majority of the lessons are taken from the NIV however there are a few that are of the NKJV. It is not to say one is better over the other, it is merely because I chose to teach on that particular version given the wording it used. Regardless of the version you personally use, you can still be successful in this study.

At the end of each lesson is something called "This Week's Extra Tid-Bit(s)." This is some little extra token or nugget of information usually having something to do with the week's lesson. It is an extra piece of encouragement. Sometimes it is an extra verse, a song to listen to, poem, or a quote by someone such as CS Lewis or Spurgeon. I hope you take note of these extra tid-bits and find encouragement in them.

Preface

This study guide is here, it is real, and it is tangible because God is good.

For the past two to three years I have gone through a whirlwind of emotions and circumstances in my life. Nothing traumatic or crisis-like. But, stressful and overwhelming, nonetheless. I was homeschooling our two oldest children, and had a two year old in tow also. I was working full time in addition to homeschooling. I worked from home, which was both ideal and a potential source of stress and chaos. I was free to be home with my children most of the time, however, that meant finding the right balance and time to complete my everyday tasks for work. Additionally, my husband dealt with a couple medical issues during this time, which added unknown variables. Thank the Lord, those issues are now under control. Throughout all this, and some other details, I became very overwhelmed. I found myself not listening to the Lord as much. And when I heard him, I brushed it off with excuses. This was nothing that was done intentionally, I knew I was doing it, in my heart I didn't want to ignore the Lord but it became easier to just go about my business. The busyness of life, family matters, work and homeschooling just consumed me. I started to put God on the backburner. I was so focused on getting to my computer in the evening to complete some work that my son would ask to say bedtime prayers and I began to shove it to the side. I began rushing them to bed, ignoring his request because I had work to do. Here is my, then four year old son asking to pray with me and I said, "Later" or "You can pray on your own tonight." When I realized I was doing this, it crushed me. My number one job God has given me is to be a mother and caregiver to my family - my husband and kids. Sure, I can be other things and I am, but the priority he set before me is to be a wife and mother. I felt like I was failing.

In the past, approximately five months, before this study guide was finished being written, we moved. Not down the street, or to the next town, but to a different state, several states away. Many reasons for this, but after doing so, I had come to a place of needing to reconnect with the Lord. The past two to three years in addition to moving led me to a place of needing rest, needing to fellowship with God again. Understand, I wasn't some full blown rebel, denying my faith and turning my back on Jesus. No, this is all very subtle. I still went to church, still prayed, and still fellowshipped with believers and friends, still taught in the Children's Ministry. But, I was getting the sense that I was going through the motions and had lost my real love for the

Lord. I allowed life to overwhelm me, which it does when our eyes aren't on the Lord and our priorities become skewed.

As I began to regain my closeness with the Lord, I knew I needed to get into devotions daily. This sounds easy and for anyone who has been a Christian for any length of time, knows this is a typical way to learn about the Lord and prepare for your day. Nonetheless, it is difficult when you have a hectic schedule so I hadn't been doing it. I knew that not reading God's Word every day and learning from him was contributing to the way I had been feeling. So, I began devotions. As I did, I felt the need to write out some of my thoughts during these devotions, thinking it would help me study. It did, but that didn't quite cut it, so I began writing a blog with these thoughts; things the Lord was speaking to me, really. Though, I liked doing the blog, it didn't cut it either. So, I began writing these lessons the Lord was showing me out in the style more like a lesson, with a little more formality to it. All the while praying and asking God to work through me, I began turning these lessons he was showing me into this study guide.

Understand, each lesson, each week's topic is directly something the Lord has been speaking to me about. I say this because I want all readers and partakers of this study guide to understand it's real. It's coming from a place of understanding and empathy through experience to what the reader might be going through. This is simply because God is good. He is working in me and because of that I pray he would work through me as well. I pray he will use the lessons I needed (and still need) to learn to help encourage you and help you grow in the Lord.

About the Author

Jennifer has been a believer, a person who believes solely in the Lordship and saving grace of Jesus Christ for salvation, since she was an adolescent. She was born in and grew up in California. She realized her need for a savior at the age of twelve. And thus, a journey of a lifetime began in Christ. Throughout the years, God has brought her up and matured her in him. She is not complete yet and nor will she be until he returns or takes her home. However, she has learned a lot and has grown in him in many ways over the course of the years.

She has been married to her husband Allen for fourteen years and they have three young children. By profession she has been a teacher for eleven years. God has blessed her with a wide range of experience in different school settings which has brought her an extensive variety of knowledge and experience as to how different school systems operate as well as what really works, what helps students learn, and in what environments. She has worked in public schools, a private school, a site based charter school as well as a home based charter school. In 2010 she completed her Master's in Education having studied Curriculum and Instruction. All of her education and experience as a teacher has well prepared her for writing Bible Studies, as it in of itself is a curriculum.

Just before writing this study guide she moved with her husband and children to Texas. A big move that provided many new opportunities. She continues to reside in Texas and is enjoying her time in a new season of life. She is eager to share the Lord and teach about him and his redemptive love that is for all mankind through writing. Making a decision for Christ is the most important decision anyone can and will ever make. She is humbled that God would lead her, guide her, and equip her in whatever type of teaching she does; whether it be with her children, in a classroom or as a writer. It is not of anything she has done but only by his grace and glory that she succeeds in her endeavors.

In her spare time she enjoys the ocean, thunderstorms, road trips, hikes, exploring new places, the ukulele, good food (especially tacos from "the taco truck"), family and friends.

Part 1

Understanding the Foundation and Essentials of Christianity: Reflection

Lesson 1 (Week 1)

The Cross: Its Effect on the Veil and What it Means for Me

When most people hear the word "veil" they would most likely think of a wedding veil. A piece of fabric that the bride wears in front of her face to hide her face until her newly pronounced husband removes it upon marriage. That would be a correct definition of a veil, however, the one we are about to study is of a different type; though a wedding veil is a symbolic gesture that ties into the veil of this lesson. This veil was altered considerably because of the cross and is the most important kind of veil and understanding it will change your life!

Day 1 - Read Matthew 27:11-26 NIV

In this passage, Jesus is on earth, fully human and fully God. He is about thirty-three years old. He's traveling and teaching wherever he goes. At this time, in this region Pilate was governor. He had two prisoners: Jesus Barabbas and Jesus the Messiah. Jesus Barabbas was a criminal. Jesus the Messiah had never been charged with a crime, never committed any act worthy of death or even the slightest punishment. Yet, when Pilate gave the people a choice as to which should be let go and who should be punished, they chose Jesus the Messiah to be held. He would be crucified. Pilate did not agree. He actually didn't want to sentence Jesus the Messiah, but he gave the people what they wanted. He took some water and washed his hands clean, declaring he has nothing to do with this crucifixion then Pilate handed him over.

Sometimes in scripture there are repeated words or phrases to show emphasis or simply because God knows we need to hear it more than once. Are there any repeated words or phrases that might show importance?

Why do you think the people choose Jesus and not Barabbas?

Was Pilate right to give the people what they wanted even if it meant killing an innocent man? Why or why not? Explain.

Pilate washed his hands of this crucifixion, but is he still responsible for it since he was in authority? Why or why not? Explain.

Day 2 – Read Matthew 27: 27-44 NIV

Jesus took on the most brutal beating imaginable. People mocked him. Slandered his name. They placed a crown of thorns on his head to mock his Kingship. These thorns were not small ones you may prick your finger on in your garden. It is said they were multiple inches long. They took his clothes off and put a scarlet robe on him. They spit on him. Then they led him, while he carried his own cross, to the place he'd be crucified. There, with two other people, whom were actually criminals, they crucified him. As brutal as all this sounds when you read the account, it still lessens the intensity knowing someone else was driving those nails in him. But, have you ever stopped to think why they were doing that? Yes, it's because he was punished to death on a cross on Pilate's orders, but it goes deeper than that. He's there to take on the sin of the world. That makes it a little more personal. He wasn't just dying for the people of the day. He was dying for all the people of the world, all that would ever live. But, wait, let's make it even more real. He was dying for *you!* Yes, you! You put him there! Now that's a dose of reality. You're reading day two of week one in this study guide and I just said something that's about as real as one can get. If you could hear my voice say this you'd know I'm not being harsh, mean, or insensitive. I'm being truthful. This is the most fundamental, basic truth there is in all of the world. You are a sinner as am I. We all are. In order for our sin to be forgiven he paid for it. He went to the cross to give his life in order that you may have everlasting life with him. So you see, you (and I) put him on that cross. It is *your* sin and *my* sin very specifically as the reason he was there. He did it for each individual person that has ever lived and ever will live. We must remember the price that was paid. It was not an easy one and it was the ultimate one. John 15:13 (NIV) says,

"Greater love has no one than this: to lay down one's life for one's friends."

That's what Jesus did; laid his life down for us.

Who actually crucified him? Not literally who was there driving in the nails, but who was he paying for?

Name two things the people shouted at Jesus while he was on the cross.

What was the significance/symbolism of the scarlet robe?

What was the place called where they led him to in order to be crucified? What do you think is the significance in this name?

Day 3 – Read Matthew 27:45-55 NIV

The veil was a tall, estimated at about sixty feet high (according to Jewish tradition), curtain hanging in the temple. Because of the separation man had from God because of sin, no one could go pass the curtain or veil except the high priest and only once a year. This veil was so thick that nothing could tear it apart; approximately four inches thick or the breadth of a man's hand (according to Jewish tradition). At the last breath on the cross, after many hours of brutal beatings, mocking and unbelievable pain Jesus cries out and gives up his spirit (v.50 NIV). At that moment the work on the cross was finished. What the cross meant to do was to remove the punishment of death for every human who lived and ever would live. See, Jesus was a perfect man, no crime, no bad deeds, no sin. Even so, it was necessary for him to go to the cross, and he knew it and he was willing to do so even knowing what it would cost. It was necessary because we were the imperfect ones. He did it for us, not himself; he didn't need it, but we did! Because of this, at that moment he yielded up his spirit. As he did, there was a great earthquake and the rocks split opened. Even the earth trembled and recognized what happened. Perhaps the greatest thing that resulted of this one particular moment was that the four inch think, sixty foot tall veil that no one and nothing could tear apart.....*Tore!* Right down the middle, just ripped straight through from top to bottom (v.51 NIV). This is amazing. This is the defining moment in history that completely changed everything. Before the veil was torn, we were separated from God. We would never be able to enter in his presence because of our sin. Sin can't mix with holiness. Just as dark can't mix with light. God loved us so much that he gave his only Son (John 3:16 NIV). He gave his Son to solve this problem. Only something perfect could take something imperfect and full of blemishes and cast it on himself to make the other clean. And, that's what he did. In a modern analogy most people can probably relate to, I'll use my former pastor's analogy: what Jesus did for you on the cross so the veil could be torn was as if you had a huge financial debt. So big you'd never overcome it. Jesus went to the bank and told the teller to transfer the amount of your entire debt from his account to yours. It's done. It's paid. *You owe nothing!* It would be crazy to have that debt paid off yet never thank the one who paid it. Or, never talk to him. You'd be so excited and grateful for what he did, you'd want to tell everyone. You probably wouldn't be able to stop smiling. It would be ridiculous to think you wouldn't show some sort of gratitude for this extraordinary act that was just bestowed upon you. But, that's exactly what happens when you, I, or others don't live for God. He has paid this debt ahead of time, even before you were born knowing it would be needed. Yet, some people choose not to choose Christ. They choose to go on mocking him just as people did when he was on the cross. People continue to leave him out of their lives. How that must sadden his heart. Other implications of the veil being torn is it is a picture of God's heart breaking as his only Son dies. The earth shakes and rocks split all because God in heaven has given his Son for all mankind. But, God being so loving to his people, knew it had to be done and in his moment of grief knew there would be greatness to come.

What are the keywords in the scripture reading?

Jesus dying on the cross means our debt has been paid. What physically happened when he gave up his spirit?

Why would the earth shake and rocks split?

What is the symbolism and importance of the veil being torn?

Why do some people continue to reject Jesus even when he has paid their debt? Name three reasons.

Day 4- Read John 3:16 NIV, Romans 6:23 NIV, Romans 10:9 NIV

The cross and the veil tearing because of the finished work of the cross have many life changing applications. Many were discussed in yesterday's lesson. The final point is this: with the veil being torn down, it is now open of *all* persons who ever are born of this earth, not one culture, not one country, not one political affiliation, but *all*. He died for *all*. Just as when you are given a gift, you have the choice as to whether or not you accept it, but if you do, you receive it without payment. When someone is genuinely giving you a gift you have the choice to take it, however, it's only right that you do. In fact, in some cultures, if you don't it's considered an insult. Once you've accepted the gift, you don't take it and then spend the rest of your life trying to pay for it in some way so that you've earned it. It's a gift. It is given to you because someone loves you. You take a gift, you choose to receive it. A gift being given to you is not because you have done something, it is because someone loves you and thought of you. You don't have to earn a gift; that would be a reward. So it is with Jesus. His dying on the cross for you is a gift because he loves you. You can't earn it. You can't be good enough. You just receive. And when you do receive it and confess it, what you're doing is accepting the fact that your debt is paid, that your sin is forgiven and gone! Remember what I said before…sin can't mix with holiness. Well, guess what? Once you do accept Christ's gift, believe upon him and repent, your sin is gone. That's right. You can now "mix" with God. He can now come into your life and start leading you *to* many blessings and *through* the hard times. You can now have a relationship with him. You will still sin, but you are forgiven and you are constantly being shaped into a Godlier person. The veil, like the one at a wedding, kept us from seeing the Father, just as a wedding veil keeps the bride hidden from the groom. When that wedding veil is removed, there is cause for a great celebration and they have declared to be together always. That's the reality of the veil in the temple. It was there because we could not be in the presence of God. Once it was removed, it is cause for celebration and God has vowed to have us in his eternal Kingdom, should we choose to repent of our sins and accept the gift.

What's the keyword in John 3:16 (NIV) that shows he died for *all*?

What's God's gift to us?

Do you have any responsibility in how you live your life once you've received this gift? If so, what should you be doing?

Day 5 – Read Matthew 27: 11-55 NIV,
John 3:16 NIV, Romans 6:23 NIV, Romans 10:9 NIV

Now that you've read through the crucifixion and what it means for the veil in the temple, reflect on what the Lord teaches us in this section of scripture.

What has the Lord revealed to you personally in this week's lesson?

What are two key points to take from this lesson?

This Week's Extra Tid-Bit:

"Therefore, brothers, since we have confidence to enter the Most Holy Place by the blood of Jesus, by a new and living way opened for us through the curtain, this, his body…" Hebrews 10:19-20 NIV

This Week's Prayers:

_____
_____
_____
_____
_____
_____
_____
_____
_____
_____
_____
_____
_____
_____
_____

This Week's Praises and Thanksgiving:

_____
_____
_____
_____
_____
_____
_____
_____
_____
_____
_____
_____
_____
_____

Lesson 2 (week 2)

Jesus Overcame So You Could Overcome

Last week you learned about the death of Jesus on the cross and how the veil, which symbolically and physically separated people from the presence of God, was torn; restoring our ability to have a relationship with him. Well, that's only half the story. If Jesus died on the cross as payment for our sins, what next? Why did that need to happen? We know it happened so our sin is paid but what good is it, is that where it all ends? What makes his death different? Why can't just anyone just claim to have the ability to pay for all mankind's sins? It's what happens next that answers these questions.

Day 1 – Read Luke 23:50-55 NIV

First, a man named Joseph came to bury the body of Jesus. This was a man that did not agree with the crucifixion. In fact he had become a follower of Jesus. Matthew 27:59 (NIV) says in reference to Joseph,

> "…who had himself become a disciple of Jesus."

He took Jesus off the cross and wrapped him in the linens that was custom of the day. They placed him in a burial area, the tomb, rolled a huge boulder in front of it so nothing such as animals or thieves could get in. The boulder weighed approximately anywhere from one to three tons. The weight alone would probably keep anything from getting in but Roman guards also sealed it to be sure (Matthew 27:66 NIV). The custom concerning Jewish tombs at this time was to put several bodies in the same tomb, so they were built fairly big compared to our modern "hole in the ground" for one casket. This tomb was different. This tomb had not been used. It had no other bodies in it and never had previously. Perhaps that says something about Jesus. Grief stricken Mary and Mary Magdalen went home and prepared spices and other things customary to their traditions to bring to the tomb. This was all in preparation for the next day. They could not prepare the following day because it would be the Sabbath and they observed the Sabbath by not doing any work.

How might have Joseph and others felt as Jesus was being wrapped in linens? List some emotions.

How did you/do you feel the first time you learned of the crucifixion?

If Jesus *had* to die, as it was the only way, in order to take on himself the world's sin, was it right for Pilate, Joseph and others who didn't want him crucified to feel that way? Or should they have been ok with it? Is it just emotions? Did they know their sin was being paid by this act?

What might have been the significance/symbolism be of this tomb not having any other bodies in it? What does this say about Jesus?

Is it important we observe the Sabbath just as the women did? Why or why not? Explain.

Day 2 – Read Luke 24:18 NIV

In yesterday's lesson we saw the events of taking Jesus off the cross, wrapping him in linens and placing him in the tomb. This is the first day. The second day, there is no doubt a sense of mourning and grief but nothing happens; nothing out of the ordinary. On the third day after he died, two grief stricken women went to the tomb early in the morning to take spices, a customary gift. This was Mary, the mother of Jesus, and Mary Magdalen. When they got there, they were shocked at what they saw! The boulder was rolled away. How was this possible? It weighs somewhere between two thousand and six thousand pounds and it was sealed. Even more shocking, Jesus was not in the tomb! Luke 24:4 (NIV) tells us two men had suddenly appeared. They were wearing shining garments and appeared to have authority. The women were frightened and startled so they bowed. The men said to them in verse 5 of Luke 24,

"Why do you look for the living among the dead?"

The men went on to say he isn't here but has risen! Then, in verse 7 (NIV), the women recalled Jesus speaking to them in Galilee saying,

"'The Son of Man must be delivered into the hands of sinful men,
be crucified and on the third day be raised again.'"

Suddenly it all made sense. Can you imagine the look on the women's faces as they remembered those words from Christ? Pure astonishment, relief, and excitement.

What's the explanation for the boulder being moved? How is it possible?

Who might these men be? Explain.

List some emotions and thoughts that you think were going through the women when the realized this was all prophesied and come to pass.

Day 3 - Read Luke 24:9-35 NIV

Rushed with excitement, the women went back and told everything to the apostles. The apostles didn't believe them, however. It couldn't be true! There's no way anything could get in *or* out of the tomb! But Peter, good ol' Peter, ran over to the tomb. When he looked in, it was true! No Jesus. He left wondering what had happened. A little disappointed and sad I imagine. The scripture goes on to tell us that two of the apostles were walking and talking about all the events that have happened when Jesus appeared to them but they had no idea it was him. Does this ever happen to us, as believers? Are we ever upset about something and Jesus is right there in the midst trying to show himself and we don't see him? We have to be careful not to miss the blessing in the trial. It's easy to do. In a trial we tend to be down cast and melancholy, wondering why it's happening to us. But Jesus is right there. He *is* the blessing. Don't miss the blessing. Finally, the time came in which they recognized him. He sat down to eat with the two that had been walking and as Jesus broke bread and gave thanks their eyes were opened; they realized who he was, but he disappeared. They got up and went to tell the others. Do you tell others? When your eyes were opened and you saw Christ clearly, did you want to tell people? It's a natural response to want to share Jesus with others once we've seen him for who he really is for the first time as people tend to be overcome with joy and excitement. There's an excitement and a sense of amazement when we come to realize the truth of Jesus. Hold on to that. All too often, it becomes easy to lose the excitement once we've known Jesus for some time. Not because he's not exciting, not because he isn't still our Savior, but because we lose sight of him. We can let life get in the way. We put him on the backburner.

Are you at a point in your life in which you see Jesus clearly? Or is there something preventing you from seeing him? Explain.

Have you ever missed the blessing of Christ because you were too stuck on what went wrong? Elaborate.

Jesus had taught his followers that he must be crucified and raised in order for others to enter his glory. Why were they so down cast when he was buried?

How can you be sure you don't doubt? How can you be sure you stay focused on the Lord and believe his word?

Day 4 – Read Luke 24:36-53 NIV

Once again Jesus appeared, this time to all of the disciples. Right away they were thinking that they must be seeing a ghost. Jesus knowing their thoughts asks them why they are frightened. In verse 38-39 (NIV) he says to them,

"'Why are you troubled, and why do doubts rise in your minds? Look at my hands and feet. It is I myself! Touch me and see, a ghost does not have flesh and bones, as you see I have.'"

They still did not believe so he continue to teach them and make himself known to the disciples. Finally, they understood and he was taken up into heaven as he blessed them. This is so amazing. Jesus comes to us over and over again. He keeps knocking. Just as he did here with his disciples. It took several times of seeing him, even seeing his scarred hands and feet, and they still didn't believe. But Jesus never gets mad and leaves or gives up on them. He continues to make it known who he is through ways the disciples can understand. It's the same for you and me. He doesn't give up on us. Sometimes doubt creeps in. Sometimes, we've seen Christ, we know Christ but we still struggle to believe what he says. More on this to come in next week's lesson about having true faith. So for now, take comfort in knowing Jesus loves you more than anything. His love for you is unconditional, even on the days you have a hard time and doubt makes its way in. Just stick with him as the disciples did. He kept teaching them and they kept listening. Jesus will speak, if you ask him and desire to hear from him. Be sure you're listening!

Have you had doubts creep in? If so, why does this happen?

What are some of the ways you address the issue when this happens?

When did the disciples go from doubt to belief?

Day 5 – Read Luke 23:50-24:1-53 NIV

The first week of this study you looked at the crucifixion and the veil; a price that was paid. This week you've looked at the burial, resurrection and ascension. This is one big event that we broke down into two weeks. What compliments the first half of the story with the crucifixion and the veil is the fact that he rose. Remember some questions I proposed at the beginning of the week? If Jesus died on the cross as payment for our sins, what next? Why did that need to happen? So our sin is paid but what good is it? Is that where it all ends? What makes his death different? Why can't just anyone suffer a horrible death (and some do) and say they paid for sin and their sin is no longer upon him? Is it a bit clearer now? The reason his death is different is because he rose! He did not stay in the tomb. Death did not win. He defeated death! That's what makes him different than just anyone dying. We all die, but none of us rise under our own power. Other gods have died and none have risen. Presidents die, but none have risen. Jesus rose and is alive because he is the one and only God. He overcame what can't be overcome. The women, who went to visit the tomb that morning did not go expecting for Jesus to be alive. They were grieving and they were hurt. But, these women now had a reason to rejoice. Jesus's resurrection takes away our sorrow. We have a reason to be joyful as well. There are times we are all in the midst of something hurtful or painful, but it is only for a time. Because Jesus rose from the grave, he conquered death. When you put your trust and life in his hands, his righteousness gets transferred to you. Because he defeated death, you too, can have the benefits of his defeating death. Not only do you defeat the troubles of this world, but you receive everlasting life with him, not eternal death. Life is hard and will continue to be hard even as a believer. However, with him working in and through you whatever it is that is bothering you or tearing you up, Jesus has already conquered. The battle has already been won! Abide in him, let him fight your battles and know that you are loved.

Now that we've looked at the full death and resurrection of Christ, take a look inside yourself and ask whether or not you've accepted the gift of your debt being paid and having eternal life.

Have I accepted his gift? Circle yes / no

If so, am I living as though I've accepted this gift? What's one way Christ has changed me?

If not, do I want to? Circle yes / no

If yes, say this prayer and let someone know so they can help foster your new relationship with Christ.

Prayer: Dear Jesus, I realize that I am a sinner in need of a Savior. I believe you died on the cross to forgive my sin and pay my debt. I know because of this, the veil was torn. I believe you were raised three days later. I believe you conquered death and offer me the gift of eternal life with you. I want to accept that gift. I ask that you forgive my sin, come into my life, my heart, and change me. Come be my Lord and Savior. Thank you, in Jesus's name, Amen.

[If you said this prayer and meant it for the first time, congratulations! You now have permanent residency with Jesus for eternity. The wages of sin which is death, is no longer upon you. It's that easy. Just believing on him is what saves us. Because of that belief, though, there should be a response. You will begin to see yourself change. There will be evidence of a changed heart, so please be sure to get connected with a fellow believer right away to mentor you and be sure you're in a Bible believing and teaching church. Because of your decision, it is vital you let someone know. Not for the sake of "show" but because Jesus is going to begin working in you and you may have questions. You should begin to learn more and see what he has in store for you.]

Why did the resurrection need to happen?

What does the resurrection mean for me?

What is one area/thing I need to let Christ defeat for me? One area I am struggling? Be sure to add it to your prayer list for the week.

Listen to the song "You Are My King (Amazing Love)" several artists have recorded this song, including Newsboys

This Week's Prayers:

_____
_____
_____
_____
_____
_____
_____
_____
_____
_____
_____
_____
_____
_____
_____

This Week's Praises and Thanksgiving:

_____
_____
_____
_____
_____
_____
_____
_____
_____
_____
_____
_____
_____

Lesson 3 (Week 3)

Faith: Believe It!

What is faith? For the longest time I thought I had faith, real faith. According to my understanding of faith it was believing in something that wasn't tangible. Pretty straight forward. I can't see God physically but I believe he's real. That's the most simple way to put what I thought was faith, or having faith. If you find yourself believing that, too, take heart it is true. However, it is only one component of faith. It does support the Biblical definition of faith found in Hebrews 11, however, I found myself only believing this half way, only believing one portion of the verse, without even knowing I was missing the other portion. This week let's take a good look at what Hebrews says and reflect on your own faith. It's important to be honest. Ask the Lord to open your eyes and heart to anything that needs to be changed regarding your faith.

Day 1 – Read Hebrews 11:1 NKJV.

Work on memorizing this verse this week.

Verse 1 says,

"Now faith is the substance of things hoped for, the evidence of things not seen."

Over the next two days we will take this apart and see what it means.

"Faith is the substance of things we hoped for…"

Looking up the word "substance" online in a thesaurus, I found a great definition. It said, "Stuff." Isn't that right? Substance is stuff. It's what something is made of, the material. So whatever we hope for, faith is that stuff. Faith is made of that material. Let's take it a bit further. What is hope? In order to know what/who hope is we have to break in down more. The word "hope" is the complete assurance in something or someone. The word "hope" in its original Hebrew and Greek form means to know for sure, with certainty, no doubt. So faith is having no doubt. Faith is the stuff or the material that is in having no doubt. And yet, taking it a little further… no doubt about what? What is our faith in? God. Therefore, we have no doubt about God. We have complete assurance in the things of God. God is our hope. In him alone we can have hope. There is no hope in this world. I do not have complete assurance about anything in this world. Everything in this world is carnal. Everything in this world will one day come to an end; whether it be our lives or the physical elements of the world such as our houses, buildings, furniture, clothes, vehicles, etc…all these things die, fall apart, rot, denigrate, wither and so on. So there is no hope in these things, God is our hope. He is the only one that doesn't change but is constant.

"Faith is the substance of things we hoped for…"

Based on our analysis, faith is stuff or material made of what we have complete assurance in. And of course, we know, that is God.

Look up the word "faith" in a thesaurus…look at the first six words (synonyms). List them below and discuss (when your group meets; if you're in a group) whether they fit the description we just analyzed?

1.   4.

2.   5.

3.   6.

Do you have complete faith in Christ? Do you have complete assurance, no doubt in him? Explain one example in your life to show you do. If you don't write down how you can.

Why shouldn't we have faith in things of this world? Example – I have faith the chair will hold me up when I sit in it. Is that wrong thinking? Or is this two different kinds of faith?

Day 2 – Read Hebrews 11:1 NKJV

Work memorizing this verse this week.

If we are going to have true faith we need to know what faith is. So, yesterday we really dug into the first half of verse one, which was the portion that says,

"Faith is the substance of things we hoped for…"

We learned that this means faith is the stuff that we have complete assurance in and no doubt about it. I mentioned at the beginning of this lesson I only believed the first half of faith, if you can still consider that faith. I was ok with this portion of the scripture we studied yesterday. I was also ok with the second portion which completed the verse. That's what we'll look at today. It says it is also,

"…the evidence of things not seen."

Still talking about faith. We can't see God himself physically and he knows this. So it's addressed in this portion of the scripture. It says,

"Faith is the 'evidence' of things not seen."

In looking up this word, I found the definition to be "something that makes plain or clear." God has made himself plain and clear! If it is plain and clear then is there any who can't see it? I would suggest that it is of their own choosing if they can't see it. God has made himself and his creation simple and easy to see as well as recognizing it's his handiwork. So if one doesn't "see" it spiritually, because they see if physically, they have chosen to deny it. This is a dangerous place to be. For those, we need to pray and ask God that he'd bring them to repentance. All around us there is evidence. Nature, time, seasons, the weather, even miracles that take place. People miraculously get healed of a disease or defy the odds of walking again and so on. These aren't coincidences or things that just happened. They aren't things that happened because one was lucky enough. It's because God is evident and he's making himself known! Look around. Next time you're at a lake, pond, watching the fish, near majestic mountains, watching the snow fall, seeing a sunrise or sunset, you are in or hear a thunderstorm, those are all evidences of God's existence. So when we look at what faith is…in its entirety, it is the stuff or material of what we have complete assurance in, which is God and the plainness and clarity of his existence. When we have faith we see and believe the evidence of his existence. That's the whole verse but only the first half of having faith. Tomorrow we will look at how we put this verse into practice through our daily lives in order to really have faith.

Look up several synonyms for "evidence" and list them.

1.   4.
2.   5.
3.   6.

Do any of the synonyms appeal to you? Which one best relates to this verse and helps you "see" God the most?

What word in this verse sticks out the most to you and why? Some examples – "faith," "substance," "evidence."

Do you know someone who is denying the plain and clear examples of God in our world? Be sure to add them to your prayer list for this week.

Day 3- Read Hebrews 11:1 NKJV

Keep working on memorizing the verse

I hope over the last two days you have learned what faith is and have been encouraged. Hebrews 11:1 (NKJV) is not lacking in its definition of faith. The Bible is complete. So in today's lesson when I talk about my not having complete faith even though I believed Hebrews 11:1 (NKJV) I am not suggesting that there is more. I am merely indicating that once you know what the Bible is teaching there is a responsibility to live it out. And that's where I was lacking. And that's what I am considering the "second half" when I say I only believed half, or had half the faith I should have had.

It wasn't until I saw a poster one day, did I realize I don't have faith or at least faith as I should. It was a troubling thought. I knew Jesus as my personal Savior and Lord. Perhaps this is why it was so shocking to me when I made this realization. I don't recall exactly the saying on the poster but it was something to the effect of, "faith is not just believing *in* God, it's believing he *will do* what he said he will do." This may not seem like a big deal. And the quote may even sound simple or obvious. But the reason it hit me so hard was because I would catch myself saying, "I know God can _____ (fill in the blank), but will he?" I found myself thinking, "I know God is capable but I'm not sure he will." I wasn't thinking he wouldn't fulfill the events of the Bible such as his second coming or things like that. I fully believed those things. It was in my personal life. I know God can provide, but will he? I know he can help me talk to this person and give me the words to say, but will he? Of course he will! Over the last two days we discovered that faith is having full confidence, no doubt, and complete assurance that God is our hope as well as seeing God's works all around us and knowing of his existence because he makes himself known plainly and clearly. That's all well and good, but now what? In a later lesson we will discuss knowledge in depth. We will learn about head knowledge vs. experiential knowledge. So forgive me for jumping ahead, but that's the concept we have in front of us now. We can know what faith is, we can even claim to have faith. But what good is it if it's not lived out? Maybe an even more important question would be is that really even faith? Maybe. I knew Jesus before I had this realization, and in order to know him I needed faith. The Bible says in Galatians 2:16 (NIV) that we are justified by faith. When a person gives their life to Christ they are justified. And so, since I knew the Lord, I was justified, which means I had faith. But, is it possible to have faith and not know the full extent or be living it out? These are questions that I hope if you are in a group you will discuss. If you are doing this individually I hope you will think on them and search scriptures for more answers and be in prayer about it. I felt that my faith was incomplete, not because of my lack of faith, but because of my lack of living it out. I had it, but now I was responsible to act like it, live by it, show it. So in thinking these like I mentioned before…I know God can, but will he? I was lacking in the "…but will he" part? If he didn't fulfill whatever the "will he" part is, I was making God a liar. To make one thing clear, God is not a liar! He is incapable of sinning. So it was purely my doing. My sin in making God seem that way. It wasn't really so. I know God can provide, but not sure if he will. That's a contradictory statement and yet this was my thought. If God said he will, then he will. I know God can, he's capable of giving me the words to witness to that person, but will he? *Yes!* He said he would, therefore he will! Don't make God out to be a liar as I did. Now, everything is in God's timing and how he sees fit. So, he may provide at a time that is different than you'd like or he may give you words you didn't plan on saying or at a different time than you thought. But, it's his timing and in his way. So, yes, he will give you what you need. He will do what he said he will do. This is a valuable lesson that makes faith complete.

Fill in the blank….

I know God can _____ and I know *he will* according to his will.

I know God is capable of _____ and I know *he will* according to his will.

It can be scary to think you have made God out to be a liar sometimes because you want to honor the Lord. It was for me. It wasn't my intension, but nevertheless, essentially it's what I was doing. Can you think of a time in the past or maybe even now that you have made God out to be a liar (which of course, he's not, but that's what your actions showed)?

Search the scriptures and find someone who made God out to be a liar. Maybe someone who didn't really believe or doubted. How did he/she do this?

In reference to Jesus's testimony, what does John 3:33 say?

Day 4 - Review Hebrews 11:1 NKJV

Hopefully, by now this verse is beginning to stick and
you about have it committed to memory.

Yesterday's lesson was about not making God a liar and believing him to be who said he is which means he will fulfill everything he said and will do what he said. I used my own previous thoughts as examples. As stated before I was bewildered at the notion that I didn't have faith, at least completely. I was bothered that I was making God a liar and that I wasn't trusting him whole heartedly. Something else that bothered me was how was I thinking this? I know Jesus as my Savior, I go to church, I pray and so on. It's not like I had abandoned my faith. So, how did I not have a complete faith?

Well, there could be many reasons. One could be we all are in a process of growing (or should be). We don't learn everything about God instantly upon becoming a Christian. He is always working in us. So maybe I just hadn't reach that point yet. Another is none of us are perfect. I just had sin that needed to be taken care of and thanks be to God for exposing it so I could repent and move forward. Still another could be, no matter what I was doing on the outside such as the things listed above, it's the inside that can "make or break" us. Sometimes the enemy just wants to get a foot hold on our lives. He doesn't need much. Just a crack in the door so-to-speak and he can begin to pry it open. This is done subtly so we may not even notice at first. It's possible he began to plant seeds of doubt in a very subtle manner. So subtle I didn't even notice it at first, I just started thinking the "...but will he" statements. We should not give so much attention to the devil that our focus is always on him, but we do need to know he is very real with a very real agenda to keep you from Christ. So be aware of your circumstances and what's going on. Be aware of your actions and reactions to situations. How does the Lord want you to react in comparison to how the devil wants you to react? Needless to say, from that day on when I saw that poster I had a new outlook on my own faith. I now knew and had every confidence to know of God's existence and everything that it encompasses, including he will do what he said he will do. Be sure you are right in your faith. If you find you are lacking ask the Lord to give it to you. Ask him to give you the faith you need. Put it on your prayer list and remember the rest of this week. He is faithful to equip you. What a trustworthy and faithful God!

Has the enemy tried to get a foot hold on your life recently? Write it out here and ask the Lord to help you.

Knowing what faith is in a deeper way, how can this help you in your own walk with the Lord?

Having studied faith in depth this week, how can this help you share Christ with others?

Day 5 – various Psalms based on search

I hope this week's lessons have made you think. I hope you've learned something about faith and your faith has been enriched. Remember, none of us are perfect and we are constantly being molded in the person God has designed us to be. So, if you find yourself currently in a state of uncertainty in regards to your faith or you just don't understand it as much as you thought you did, ask him to guide you. We never need to let ignorance be intimidating. It's a chance to learn and have Jesus be your teacher. He longs for you to know him more so just ask. Wrap up this week by searching the Psalms and see what's in store.

Search the Psalms for verses on faith. Read several verses and jot them down. Discuss/explain.

What's the biggest thing you feel God has spoken to you this week about your own faith?

What's one way you can and will implement something in your life to have greater faith?

This Week's Extra Tid-Bit:

"Oh, brethren, be great believers! Little faith will bring your souls to heaven, but great faith will bring heaven to you." ~C.H. Spurgeon

This Week's Prayers:

_____
_____
_____
_____
_____
_____
_____
_____
_____
_____
_____
_____
_____
_____
_____

This Week's Praises and Thanksgiving:

_____
_____
_____
_____
_____
_____
_____
_____
_____
_____
_____
_____
_____
_____
_____
_____
_____

Lesson 4 (Week 4)

Faith Assured

Sometimes we can think we know something, but in reality we don't. Sometimes we can think we have faith, but when something goes wrong we tend to question it. This week we'll look at faith on an even deeper level than last week and learn how you can be confident in it. This week's lesson is really an extension of last week's about faith as well as the first two lessons about the Jesus's death (effects on the veil) and resurrection. There may be times in which the text is referred back to a previous lesson to further the lesson.

Day 1 – Read Hebrews 10:22 NKJV

Franny J. Crosby wrote the lyrics to the hymn "Blessed Assurance." It was written in 1873. While I love Contemporary Christian music, I also love a lot of the old hymns. There is a lot we can learn from the lyrics of these hymns. We can learn about people's hearts and relationship with Jesus from these songs. In all our modern songs, technologies and the like, it is good to remember the "classics," the hymns. When Crosby wrote this song she took the lyrics in context from Hebrews 10:22 (NKJV) which says,

"…let us draw near with a true heart in full assurance of faith, having our hearts sprinkled from an evil conscience and our bodies washed with pure water."

The first part says,

"Let us draw near…"

This is an invitation. It is saying to come close, be closer. It's an action that is voluntary. This is not a command. A command may be written something like, "You must draw near…" or "You will draw near…" Neither of those are what it says. It says,

"Let us…"

So this is an invitation, like someone's hand is extended out to you asking you to come. When you have an invitation, someone thought of you. They wanted you to come or you wouldn't have received the invitation. Think of a birthday invitation or a wedding invitation. You are invited because the host wanted you there to help celebrate the event. There is a connection between you and the host. You know each other and there is some form of relationship. So, it is with the Lord. He has invited us into a relationship with him. He has invited you to draw near. He is not a distant God. He is personal and wants to be involved in your life.

When's the last time you were invited to something? How did it make you feel being invited?

How does it make you feel knowing God has invited you to draw near? Do you accept?

Right now, do you feel distant to God or close? If you feel close, what's one way you can draw nearer still? If you feel distance, there invitation still stands. What's one way you can draw near?

Day 2 – Read Hebrews 10:22 NKJV

Yesterday, we discovered Hebrews 10:22 is actually an invitation. It's inviting us to draw near or close. Today we will discuss one of two ways in which we are to draw near.

The first part of the verse says,

"Let us draw near <u>with a true heart</u> in full assurance of faith…"

So the first way to draw near is with a true heart. The second is in full assurance of faith and we'll discuss that one tomorrow.

"With a true heart…,"

means with an honest heart, it means with a committed heart and it means with a correct heart. While this sounds easy and one might think they fit this description, we have to be careful in dealing with matters of the heart. Jeremiah 17:9 (NIV) says,

"The heart is deceitful above all things, and desperately wicked…"

Therefore we need to be focused upon the Lord. This is how we gain a true heart. Our hearts, in of themselves, are wicked, we want fleshly things and we want it now. To have a true heart, a committed heart, and pure or correct heart is to look upon the Lord and keep our sight on him. He is the one that makes us new. Think of the song, "Create in Me a Pure Heart" by Keith Green. God has to create that in us. He has to change us to give us a pure heart. We don't already have it, we were born into sin. It's important to recognize that anything good we have or are comes from the Lord and not of ourselves.

What is one way you can put into practice having a true heart?

Why is drawing closer to the Lord with a true heart important?

When one first gives their life to Christ they come as they are. It doesn't matter if they are "clean" or not, in fact it's safe to say they aren't. How is drawing closer to the Lord with a true heart different than coming to the Lord for the first time with a "dirty" heart?

Day 3 – Hebrews 10:22 NKJV

Yesterday I said there was two ways as to how to draw near to the Lord. The first we talked about yesterday was with a true heart. Today, we'll look at the second which is,

"…in full assurance of faith."

Your faith in Christ can be (should be) a sure thing. The definition of the word "full," is "containing all that can be held." There's no more room for more. It has filled in every gap and every crevasse. I really like this definition. It leaves no room for anything else. "Assurance" means "guarantee." Just like "full" is having no room for more, "assurance" is having a guarantee. It's 100 percent safe or trusted. So when we have an invitation to draw near or close we can come in full assurance. We can come trusting 100 percent, completely filled to the top, no room for any other thought or emotion, but knowing our faith is genuine and true. There's no question as to the validity of Christ and all he stands for. We can be sure, as believers, he is who he said he is. He did what he said he did and he will do what he said he will do (refer back to last week's lesson on faith). We can be sure. Having assurance is having accuracy, it's having no doubt, and it's having confidence. To clarify part of this…when I say full assurance is no doubt and full confidence, it doesn't mean there aren't times that one doesn't question something and wonder why. That's part of our nature and God knows that, he made us. So, the difference is that even when one does have questions and wonders about things he/she trusts God for the answer whether it be revealed on this earth or not until heaven. We can have questions about something, but that doesn't mean it's doubtful. I can wonder why God allowed something, but that doesn't mean my faith has been shaken. I can still have full assurance in faith even when those questions come up.

Search the scriptures and write down two people that had full assurance of faith. They had no doubt but only confidence in the Lord. Give a brief description of an example of how they had full assurance.

I mentioned one definition of "full" and "assurance," but there are many more. Look up both words and write down two more definitions for each that you think are appropriate.

Full -

Assurance –

Day 4 – Read Hebrews 10:22 NKJV

We've completed the first half of this verse.

"Let us draw near with true hearts in full assurance of faith…"

We know this verse is an invitation and we know it's because the veil was torn that we now get this invitation. We also know that we have to keep our eyes on the Lord as he is the one that gives us a true heart. Lastly, so far we've learned that in all this we have full assurance of faith. It is complete, no room left for anything else. Today we will look at the rest of the verse broken in the last two parts.

Continuing in the NKJV,

"Our hearts sprinkled from an evil conscience,"

is the next part of Hebrews 10:22. Once again, Jeremiah 17:9 (NIV) says,

"The heart is deceitful above all things, and desperately wicked…"

So, our minds, our consciences and our hearts have been touched by evil. We have a tendency to gravitate toward these things, toward evil, toward the desires of our own heart. We do this because to live in sin is much easier. More things are acceptable, one doesn't have to be as accountable and the gratification is usually instant. Sometimes we don't want to see the truth of Christ because it will expose us. It will expose the sin. If the sin is exposed it means we'll be faced with a choice, keep living in it or change. Most of us don't want to give up control, especially when we're talking about control of one's life.

The last part of Hebrews 10:22 (NKJV) says,

"…our bodies washed with pure water."

So, having come from this sinful background that all people have come from (100 percent of people), we need to be washed clean. That's what Christ does. He washes us clean of our sin. Water is needed in order to sustain life. Water is needed in order to clean something. I suppose you could try just soap but it would be thick and gloppy and probably be much more difficult to wash off. So, water is needed. Jesus is the living water (John 4:10 NIV). He says that whoever comes to him will never be thirsty again (John 4:14 NIV). Anything we do on this earth apart from building Christ's kingdom, will not satisfy. We can run after fame, status at our job, try this, try that, do this or do that. It's temporary even if we do succeed at some of these things. Even the water we physically drink is necessary, but temporary. Just hours after drinking it, it will leave your body and you have to get more as to keep up the hydration level in your body. It's only temporary. And unless we keep this cycle going, it would kill us. Jesus says the water he gives is everlasting. When we are washed with him, we are never dirty again. He forgives us and we are never going to pay for our sin. There are consequences on this earth for sin, there are consequences that are a result of our wrong doing, but our eternity has been secured. When we sum up this verse using the synopsis of it we can explain it this way: We are invited to come close to Jesus with an honest and committed heart, knowing that Christ is 100 percent true, having a background of actions against God, he washes us clean. Be sure to let Jesus wash you clean. We all have the same background of sin it just manifests in different ways. Jesus invites you to draw closer to him so he can wash you. Take hold of that.

I paraphrased John 4:10 and John 4:14. Look both verses up and write them here:

John 4:10 -

John 4:14 -

Do you find it difficult when Christ exposes your sin? Why or why not?

Why is it so hard for some people to give up control and just let God?

Day 5 – Read Hebrews 10:19-22 NKJV

Hebrews 10:19-21 (NKJV) says,

> "Therefore, brothers and sisters, since we have confidence to enter the Most Holy Place by the blood of Jesus, by a new and living way opened for us through the curtain, this, his body and since we have a great priest over the house of God..."

And then this week's verse continues it in verse 22. This is all tied together. When we talked about the veil two weeks ago we talked about a curtain, which is the veil. It tore from top to bottom upon Christ's death. It symbolizes his body being torn for us and it removes the barrier between man and God. In this week's lesson we talked about drawing near to God. We can draw near with full assurance. Why can we do this? It's simply because God made it so by sending his only Son to die on the cross. There was a time after the disobedience in the Garden of Eden that man was separated from God. Jesus dying on the cross made a way for us to be back in fellowship with God. So, because of this, verse 22 holds true. We can now draw near, in full assurance of faith. I hope the significance of the cross holds a lot of weight with you. I know it does for me. The veil is typically not discussed as much the crucifixion when being taught in churches or study groups, but I find it important. When I first heard it taught I found it brought alive the crucifixion even more than before. It made it that much more real and personable for me. I hope in these last few weeks you too, have been amazed at Jesus's sacrifice and love for us.

Wrapping up this week's lesson, what's one thing that stands out to you most, either about the verse itself, or how the Lord is growing you?

How would you describe your faith at this point? Do you have full assurance? If so, explain why? If not, explain why and what you can do to have full assurance of faith.

Be sure to look at your prayer requests for the week and pray over them one more time before you end this lesson.

Listen to "Blessed Assurance" and "Create in me a Clean Heart." If you don't have either in your collection of music, both can be easily found online. As you listen, ask the Lord to give you a clean heart and thank him for his faithfulness and giving you assurance of his presence in your life.

This Week's Prayers:

_____
_____
_____
_____
_____
_____
_____
_____
_____
_____
_____
_____
_____

This Week's Praises and Thanksgiving:

_____
_____
_____
_____
_____
_____
_____
_____
_____
_____
_____
_____
_____
_____
_____
_____

Conform or Transform

Conform and transform are two very important words that may sound similar but are actually very different. This week we will break down the words and understand the difference. We will also see what the Bible says about each and how we should respond.

Day 1-Read Romans 12:2 NIV (also read verse 1 for context)

The words "conform" and "transform" sound similar. They have the same root, "form." If we look at these words a little closer here's what we discover for the meanings. Conform, as it states in Strong's Greek Dictionary is, "assuming a similar outward form (expression) by following the same pattern (model, mold)." Keep this definition in mind this week as we are studying Romans 12:2.

Verse 2 of Romans 12 in its entirety says,

"Do not be conformed to this world, but be transformed by the renewing of your mind then you will be able to test and approve what God's will is—his good, pleasing and perfect will."

Verse 1 talked about presenting our bodies as a living sacrifice, holy and pleasing. So then, because we are to present ourselves in that way, verse two tells us two things. The first thing is what not to do and the second thing is what to do. Then it is followed by how to do it. It's comforting to have both these directives and then instruction. If the Holy Spirit, who directed the authors of the Bible on what to write, just left it at what not to do, we'd all be left hanging. When we make a mistake it shouldn't be about blame or condemnation. It should be about recognizing it and learning how to correct so it is made right and doesn't happen again. There's very little good in knowing you've done something wrong if you also don't learn how to fix it. Jesus, being the loving, gracious and all-knowing teacher that he is, doesn't just leave us hanging. He tells us what not to do, but immediately follows it with what to do, so that we may be successful in our walk. He's a kind, caring and loving God. He gives his children every opportunity to succeed. So, the first thing he tells us is not to be conformed to this world. That's what we shouldn't do. As a believer you may feel a little out of place in this world sometimes, that's ok. In fact, you're probably on the right track. We're not permanent residents here. We've heard it said that "we're just passing through." This actually comes from Philippians 3:20 (NIV), which talks about our citizenship in heaven. Our lives on earth compared to eternity are very, very, short. Another popular saying I enjoy, in fact, have on the back of my car, alludes to the fact that we are *in* this world, not *of* it. The saying is simply "not *of* this world." We can be *in* this world and do what we're called to do, but we aren't *of* it. We aren't to be part of its ways or its thinking. When something is conformed, it has been adapted to fit in, it adjusts, and it follows. We are not to be conformed to this world. Look at the definition given at the beginning of this lesson. It's, "following the same pattern." The Bible puts this in context of the world. It says,

"Do not be conformed to this world."

Therefore, we are not to follow the pattern of this world. We are not to adapt to this world. We are not to follow it.

Both conform and transform have the same root word, "form." What does "form" mean?

Are there other verses in the Bible that talks about not being conformed to this world? If so, list them and share them/read them if you are in a group study.

What are some of the ways we can so easily be conformed to this world if we're not careful?

Do you struggle with any of these ways you listed in the previous question? If so, write it out and add it to your prayer list this week.

Day 2 – Read Romans 12:2 NIV

Yesterday we looked at "conform." We discovered that it means to follow a pattern and the Bible relates it to the pattern of the world. That is the portion that tells us what *not* to do. Today we will look at "transform" and what the Lord says *to* do. "Transform," also according to Strong's Greek Dictionary is, "change *after* being with." Keep that definition in mind.

We're all still on this earth even if we aren't to conform to it…so what do we do? The second part of this verse and what to do is to "be transformed." The definition of transform is "make a thorough or dramatic change in the form, appearance or character of." We are to change our way of doing things, seeing things, how we act, etc. We are not to act like the world. The world is full of hatred, lies, deceit, thieves, etc. There are glimmers of good things on this earth. There are rainbows that can put a smile on your face, there are kind people that are willing to help you out, and there are things like puppies, babies, and all the little things that make us go, "aww." But those are *things or people* in this world. What we're talking about for the sake of the lesson is more about moral conduct and behavior. I don't discount the physical beauties of this world, but when discussing conform and transform it's more behavioral and dealing with the attitude. Tomorrow when we look at the "how to do this" we'll see that it's with the mind. Therefore we aren't talking about physical things, but things of the mind. We're not to act like the world but are to change our ways to become more Christ like. Strong's definition is interesting. It's a "change *after* being with." This change doesn't come before, it comes after. What do you suppose the change is after? After what? Write your thoughts here:

Assuming you said something like after a relationship with God, we can realize that before a relationship with God we are not transformed, we simply conform whether we realize it or not. We assimilate into this world. We go along with the pattern of it. Before knowing Christ, how could one not? It's all that person knows. He/she has not known the Lord to that point, so the world is the only other choice. Matthew 12:30 (NIV) paraphrased says, you are either for God or against him. This is not a hateful statement, it's simply you either know the Lord or you don't. So once we know the Lord, we are to be transformed. We are to change after being with the Lord. This definition is important to keep in mind also. Now that there is a change that takes place after knowing the Lord, it should be, "thorough or dramatic." That doesn't mean everything all at once will change in your life (although it could). But, there should be thorough change that is happening as the Lord begins to work on you and change you to be more Christ-like. Your attitude toward people or situations may begin to improve, you may be made whole from things like alcohol, drugs, bad language or porn. It may not be anything that "bad." It may just be a realization that you are a sinner in need a savior. That too, is a dramatic change. Just this realization and your response to Jesus in that changed your eternal address from hell to heaven; that's a dramatic change.

When you first gave your life to Christ (even if it was at the beginning of this study) what did Christ begin to change first?

How did your attitude change after knowing Christ?

Overall, looking at yourself after being with the Lord (transformed) versus before when you were following the pattern of this world (conformed) what is different? Add these to your "Praises/Thanksgivings" for the week. Share if you'd like.

Are there areas you still need to be transformed? List them and add to prayer list for this week.

Day 3 –Read Romans 12:2 NIV

After reading through the verse once, try it without looking.

Just a note about today's lesson. All parts of this study are important. All parts focus of God's word and how to live for him. But, I feel I should mention something specifically in today's lesson. If you struggle with anxiety and/or depression as I have, please read this lesson carefully, thoroughly and more than once if necessary. It is key to conquering anxiety and depression. So much anxiety is caused by worry, living things over that cause stress or living in moments that haven't happened yet that scare us (that may never happen). Please ask the Lord for help. Ask him to renew your mind and heal you from this. I am not against medical help, but I know God is the ultimate healer. God is our strength. Carry one another's burdens in your group this week and pray about this if there's anyone in your group needing help.

So far in this lesson we have looked at the differences of conform and transform. Hopefully, you have seen how each can have a part in our lives and have been able to reflect on how the Lord has transformed you.

The next part of the verse tell us *how* to be transformed and not conformed. It says,

> "…by the renewing of your mind."

It takes a change in one's thinking. Not just the things you say, but how you think. It's important to note that it's not us doing the changing. It's God in us. He gives us the power to be transformed. This is why it can only be done *after* we know him. *After* the change has taken place as it says in the definition. The change being that one now knows the Lord, one has given their life to him and has come into a relationship with him. As Christ followers we ought to have a changed heart. The Bible says we are a new creation (2 Corinthians 5:17 NIV). God makes us new when we accept him. All the things you've done or said that you thought made you unlovable or unforgiveable, God forgives and he begins to mold you into something beautiful. He casts your sin from you as far as the east is from the west (Psalm 103:12 NIV). The east and the west each are infinite. They go on forever in a separate direction never to meet. In mathematics, it's simply called a line. A line goes on without end with both points going in opposite directions. God has taken your sin, as bad or not so bad (even a "small" sin is a sin) and removed it so far from you that it can never find you again. The Lord never brings it up again. To him, it's gone. It's taken care of and you are no longer held accountable to it. If you really want to be transformed it's through the renewing of your mind. One of the ways to do this is to stop bringing up your past as a stumbling block. Stop feeling sorry for yourself. Stop making it an excuse. Yes, you sinned, yes, bad things were done to you. But in a relationship with Christ you are made new. You are forgiven. Your sin will never find you. You have the blood of Jesus that was shed as your guarantee. Not only is your sin taken care of, not only will change begin to happen, but the Lord can change you circumstances, too. He can give you wisdom, insight, and strength to handle your financial situation. He can give you the ability to overcome your anxiety. When your mind is renewed, there is a power released because the living God is at work in you. So, soak in what the Lord has done for you and don't let who you were *before* Christ define you now. It is your testimony, but let the Lord renew your mind. Then transformation can take place. Even if you think you've been a Christian for a long time, you know you are transformed, you know you are not the same person as before. Be careful you don't get to a place of being stagnant. Don't get to a place of just going through the motions. If you do find yourself there, ask for a renewing of the mind. Ask for him to continually transform you. We can't ever get to a place of "arrival" on this earth. As long as we are here, the Lord is always molding us. Talk to him, ask him to renew you mind and transform you. If you're in a group spend some time praying together when your group meets asking for renewal for one another. If you're individually completing this spend some time in the quiet today, talking and asking this of him.

It can be hard to let go of the past. List some things from your past that hold you back or perhaps things of the future that haven't even happened but cause you anxiety with all the "what if" statements. Things you need the Lord to renew your mind in, renew your thinking.

Here's some verses about renewal. Look them up and summarize them.

Psalms 23:3

Colossians 3:9-10

Titus 3:5

Day 4 – Romans 12:2 NIV

Really up to this point we've looked at only the first half of Romans 12:2 (NIV). Today and tomorrow we will look at the last half. So far we've studied,

> "And do not be conformed to this world, but be transformed
> by the renewing of your mind…"

The next part is…

> "…then you will be able to test and approve what God's will is..."

After you are transformed and have a renewed mind you can begin the next step. The first part of this part of the verse says "then." This word means only after the first part is complete. It is saying there is something that must be done first. What must be done first is everything we've talked about so far this week – be transformed, not conformed and renew your mind. Once the Lord begins to do this you can begin to see God's will. That's the reason to be transformed, to see God's will. If someone is being conformed to the world, they won't know God's will. They are not a part of God. They are a part of the world. The world is darkness and the Lord is light. Darkness and light can't mix. A popular buzz word in our time is "coexist." The problem is darkness and light can't coexist. Either darkness will overcome light or light drives out darkness. If you conform to this world it will overcome you. However, if you live in the light, the Lord, it will drive out the darkness in your life. So, by being transformed you are set up to be living for God and part of that is knowing what his will is so you can live by it. This part of the verse says,

> "…you will be able to test and approve what God's will is."

Why does it say test and approve? Can't we just take something at face value to be God's will? No. We can't and shouldn't. Not everything is God's will, even if it seems good. Going to be a missionary in a third world country is a good thing. It's something that is needed. It's even something God calls people to do. But, he doesn't call everyone to that. So, we need to test and approve God's will so we can know it's his. The enemy loves to deceive; it's one of his main games. So, in order to be sure something is God's will and not the enemy it is important we test it. How is this done? A former pastor of mine once gave this advice to this very topic.

How to be sure a major decision is God's will and not my selfish desires or that of the enemy keeping us from what really is God's will:

1) Pray
2) Search God's word
3) Seek counsel – a Godly person who is wise, who will pray for you, and who is unbiased

Those three things over a period of time will reveal if a particular decision is God's will or not. And then one can move on accordingly. The word "approved" here doesn't mean whether or not you approve his will. It's not up to us to approve it. We can choose whether or not to accept it and follow it. But, regardless, it's his will. So, "approved" simply means approved by God. It's his approved will, his best will for you.

What's one of the important reasons of making sure our mind is transformed?

Is there something you need to know God's will about? If so, write it here and commit to the 3 step outline mentioned in this lesson. Add it to your prayer list.

Has there ever been a decision you made that wasn't the Lord's will but yours? If so, what came of it? Did it go as planned?

Day 5-Romans 12:2 NIV

Today we will finish up the last part of Romans 12:2 (NIV). Yesterday's lesson was about testing and approving God's will. The last part describes God's will and says,

"…—his good, pleasing and perfect will."

There is more than one kind of will of God. There are several but the most common two that are talked about or taught is the perfect will and permissive will. The perfect will is that of his most desirable will. This will is what he desires for us, it is perfect, complete, and is the same will talked about in Romans 12:2 (NIV). The permissive will is what he allows to be done even though it may have been outside his perfect will. This will, however, is never outside of what God knows is going to happen. He knows how people will choose, how they will act, and what their priorities are. Given this, he still uses the permissive will to accomplish his perfect will. The last part of Romans 12:2 (NIV) is simply a description of his perfect will. It is good, it is pleasing, and prefect indicating there is nothing wrong with it and will ultimately bring about the most satisfaction. I pray we would all have the desire to fill his perfect will in our lives.

His perfect will is pleasing to whom?

Does "prefect" in this case mean without hardship? Without trial?

Why not just settle for his permissive will? God gives us choice. He gives us desires (not always bad, there are good desires). So, why should we seek his perfect will for our lives?

<u>*This Week's Extra Tid-Bits:*</u>

Listen to "Beautiful Things" by Gungor

Listen to "Where I Belong" by Building 429

"If you are renewed by grace, and were to meet your old self, I am sure you would be very anxious to get out of his company." — Charles H. Spurgeon

This Week's Prayers:

_____
_____
_____
_____
_____
_____
_____
_____
_____
_____
_____
_____
_____
_____
_____

This Week's Praises and Thanksgiving:

_____
_____
_____
_____
_____
_____
_____
_____
_____
_____
_____
_____
_____
_____
_____
_____

Lesson 6 (week 6)

Christ: The Solid Rock

This week is all about choices. We make them every day. Some are so minimal that we don't even realize we are making a choice. Some are very important and perhaps life changing. This week you will learn what one of the most important decisions you will ever make is and you will see the consequences, good or bad, of that decision.

Day 1 – Read Matthew 7: 24-27 NIV

We all have choices in life. We choose things every day, that we usually take for granted such as what to eat, what to wear, soda or tea, should I do laundry, do I want to go to the store or wait…on and on. The choices we make daily are almost endless. These are small choices that in the end matter, but not so much. In contrast, we also have choices that are more consequential. Some of these include: what the foundation of our household will be, our family values, what's acceptable and not acceptable, what we will base our life upon. After reading Matthew 7:24-27 (NIV), think about what Jesus says about foolish builders and wise builders.

Jesus says the wise person builds his house upon the _____. And in contrast the foolish person builds his house upon _____.

What is the definition of "foolish?"

What is the definition of "wise?"

Anyone who puts the words of Jesus into practice is compared to which man?

What happen to the house the foolish man built?

What happened to the house the wise man built?

So, just like the wise man building his house on solid ground so it could stand, how can we build our lives on solid ground to stand?

When it comes to our lives, why is it important to be like the wise man?

Day 2 – Read Matthew 7:24-27 NIV

Yesterday we looked at the verses in the passage and compared it to how we should build our lives. Today we will relate the principles of building on solid ground to living our lives. Before we do I will to relate this to a story in which just about everyone is familiar: *The Three Little Pigs.*

It may be a classic children's story but its lessons are just as much for adults as it is for kids. A quick synopsis of the story is as follows: *Three pigs each built a house. Each one built his house out of different materials. One with straw, one with sticks and one with bricks. As the big, bad wolf came and tried to blow down their house so he could get to them and have his dinner, two of the houses blew down and one stood. The brick house stood. It was the strongest. It had the best foundation to hold up the rest of the house. The two pigs that had built the houses that blew down ran over to the one with the brick house for safety. All three pigs were safe inside that brick house. It stood against the big, bad wolf. As a result, the big, bad wolf had to leave.*

In our lives we are constantly making choices as we mentioned in yesterday's lesson. Some of those choices include actions, what we do physically and some are behavior or attitude; how we act or react to situations. One can choose jealousy, bitterness, and not to forgive. But for someone who chooses those things, they will be like the pig with a straw house. It won't stand against the hard times. You don't have a sure foundation. One could choose selfish ambitions, to be a workaholic, to focus on career and just getting to the top.

This person is like the pig who built his house out of sticks. Though these characteristics are a bit stronger than that of the straw house, it's still dangerous and will eventually get blown down. For this person, they may not get blown down in their career or ambitions, but they will in their relationships. Thirdly, one can choose faith, hope, and love. This is like the pig who built his house with brick. It's solid. It's strong. One brick is up against another brick and sealed not letting anything come between to compromise the structure. Why are these choices so important for us? Just like the story, these pigs had something after them. Something that wanted to wreck their houses and ultimately eat them. We have things in life happen that are hard. Things that are unfair. Things that test us and bring us to our breaking point. Ultimately, there is an enemy out there wanting to destroy our families, our homes and you individually. If we are not grounded and secure we will be moved, we will fall, and our house will crumble.

Reflect on your life. Has there been a time you built your life out of straw? If so, what was the result?

What's worse: having a bad foundation physically (things like choosing soda instead of water, choosing to wear t-shirt instead of a jacket in snow, choosing to wait until the next rest stop instead of filling up on gas now then running on empty, etc.) or having a bad foundation in behavior and attitude (jealousy, bitterness, speaking in a way that puts people down, etc)? Are they just as important? Does one depend on the other? Discuss.

How is your "house" built now? On your own desires? The world's standards? The word of God? Explain.

When building a house out of brick, each brick is layered and sealed against the next to make it air tight and not let anything in from the outside. How does this translate into how our lives should be?

In verse 27, how did the house fall? Softly? Loudly? Gently? _____

What's the significance of this when related to our lives?

Day 3 – Continue to read Matthew 7:24-27 NIV

Today we will continue with relating Jesus's instruction on building on a solid foundation to the story of *The Three Little Pigs*. Another important element besides choices of foundation used to build their house is to point out the reaction of the pigs. The first two that got their house blown down ran to the other house for safety. If you do find yourself in a situation where the world is just eating you up, you can't seem to get it together, things are just too hard and you can't deal, run to the safe house. By the way, this will happen. No one is exempt from the trials of this world. Even the Lord said in John 16:33 (NIV),

> "I have told you these things, so that in me you may have peace. In this world you will have trouble. But take heart! I have overcome the world."

You will have trouble. Jesus has overcome the world so we can run to the Lord. He is our shelter from storms. What better place to go than to the one in whom the victory belongs? Don't sit and wallow in destruction, go get safety. When we are in the house that is strong, that has a sturdy foundation, which symbolically is the Lord, we will be safe. What was the reaction of the third pig? Did he have to go anywhere? Or was his trust in his house? He had confidence in his house. He knew he has built a house that could stand. Also, he let the other two pigs in. He was not selfish with his house, he did not harbor it for himself. This is how we are to be. We have confidence in the Lord. We know he is our safety. When we are in him we can have peace even through storms because we know in whom we trust.

A sturdy, strong house built on a sure foundation is symbolic for what/who in our lives?

Do you have peace in storms? If not, reflect on your relationship with the Lord. Is your trust fully in him?

How has Jesus overcome the world when there's still so much negativity and bad things going on? What does this really mean?

Day 4 – Read Matthew 7:24-27 NIV, Matthew 28:16-20 NIV

We must also be sharing Jesus with others. We must also show them the Good News. Jesus does not want us to sit in our own house and be idle. The world needs to know him. The Great Commission in Matthew 28 says we are to go into the world making disciples. For some, this means leaving home and going to a different country but for others it means in your own home. In your own town. There are people that need to know Jesus everywhere. We all, as believers are to take part in the Great Commission. And finally, arguably, most joyful part of the story is at the end. The wolf left! He realized there was no way of getting in that house. He was no match for the house. The house was stronger than he. So he retreated. This is how it is with our relationship to the enemy when we're in the Lord. When we resist the enemy's temptations, he has to flee. It may be tempting to build out of straw or sticks; after all it's quicker, easier to handle because it's not as heavy and costs less. But when one listens to the Lord, submits himself to the Lord, abides in the Lord, one gains strength to resist the devil's temptations, so the enemy flees (James 4:7 NIV). Light drives out darkness.

In Matthew 28:16-20 (NIV), there are 4 things listed of what we should do to fulfill the Great Commission. What are they?

1.
2.
3.
4.

Are you sharing Jesus as you should or do you harbor him in your own safe house?

What hinders you from sharing Jesus more? How can you overcome this?

Day 5– Review Matthew 7:24-27 NIV

This week we've looked at a fun children's story and related it to Matthew 7: 24-27 (NIV). Even though it's a fun story that kids love, it has many implications and comparisons that we can relate to Jesus's teaching in the passage for this week. The main one being Jesus is the rock and we need to build our life upon him. Be the wise one, not the foolish one. When the storms come you will be comforted, you will have hope, and you will have peace and protection. Don't be caught in a storm without shelter. Don't go through this life without the Lord. Had those first two pigs stayed in their houses made of straw and sticks, the wolf would've blown their house down and had a full belly. He would have destroyed them. So it is with life without Christ (Romans 6:23 NIV). Some people may seem to be doing fine. They're successful, are "good" people, but that's just as good as dead. The devil is happy to let you be successful in life so long as you are not living for the Lord. Don't be deceived. Keep your eyes on the Lord.

Look up Romans 6:23 and write it here:

What does "wages" mean?

Is it possible to live a "good" life without Christ? Think about the meaning of "good." Discuss.

This Week's Extra Tid-Bits:

If you want, for fun, read "The Three Little Pigs" and as you do keep in mind Jesus's teaching.

Listen to the song, "On Christ the Solid Rock I Stand" lyrics originally by Edward Mote

Listen to the song, "In Christ Alone" by Keith Getty and Stuart Townend

This Week's Prayers:

_____
_____
_____
_____
_____
_____
_____
_____
_____
_____
_____
_____
_____
_____
_____
_____
_____

This Week's Praises and Thanksgiving:

_____
_____
_____
_____
_____
_____
_____
_____
_____
_____
_____
_____
_____
_____
_____

Part II

Living it Out: Staying Steadfast While Growing in the Lord

Congratulations! You've gone through the first six weeks of this Bible study and completed Part I. You've studied the essential decisions and choices for Christianity –analyzing your relationship with Christ and understanding it. Some of it may have seemed juvenile, obvious or "old news" to those of you who have known Christ for some time, but it's an important reflection that is necessary especially knowing God's word and truths are always relevant to our lives. Sometimes we can get to a place in our relationship with the Lord in which we forget our first love as it states in Revelation 2:4. So, we need to be reminded of the foundation of our faith which consists of the information you have just studied the last six weeks. Sometimes we need to remember the basic elements of our faith for another reason, too. We can know Christ, be living for him and see him working in and through us, but all it takes is one little distraction, self-doubt, or trial to come along and we before we know it, we have strayed, we are just going through the motions, or have altogether let our relationship with the Lord go. So, we come back, readjust and get back on track.

Part II takes what you've just studied for the past six weeks and gives some key truths and applications as to how to live out your faith, be steadfast, refreshed and reconnected to the Lord in a deeper way. It gives important truths on what we need to do in order to keep our relationship with Jesus at the forefront of our priorities. The reason for this is because life is hard. Life seems unfair, life can hurt and we even make bad decisions or "fall off the band wagon" sometimes. So, for the next nine weeks focus in on Jesus and these key truths and applications. I pray that you grow in the Lord and by the end you feel renewed, revitalized and stronger in the Lord.

Lesson 7 (Week 7)

Be a Servant

Perhaps one of the most fascinating parts of scripture for me is that of the foot washing done by Jesus. It's so intricate with all the application of Jesus washing Peter and Peter having a conversation about it with Jesus. Peter is so relatable that it seems many people can see similar characteristics in Peter as themselves. So, we can learn a lot from this conversation. If you have ever wanted to know what a servant looks like, here it is! And by a king, no less!

Day 1 – Read John 13:1-5 NIV

Jesus's time on Earth was about to end but this was no news to him. Before, the events that are about to happen take place, Jesus has one last meal with his disciples. While this last meal was taking place Jesus does something so remarkable, it's unlike any other king. This section of scripture has impacted my life so much as a believer that I don't want you to miss it! You will truly be in awe of our Lord. Read John 13:1-5 carefully.

It states in verse 5 (NIV) that he poured water in a basin and started washing the disciples' feet! Let's think about this… The feet of people when Jesus was on earth were really dirty all the time. They wore sandals and walked on roads that were dusty. No doubt that as they walked several miles, especially when traveling, dirt was kicked up everywhere, not on purpose but just because of the nature of walking on a dirt road. Because of this, it was customary in this day that the guest's feet would be washed as they entered the home. The person that had this job was the lowliest of the household or the servant.

We know because of descriptions as to where Peter was sitting that, on the night of the last meal, this should have been done by Peter. But, Jesus gets up and washes their feet. Why did Jesus do this? Was he just sick of waiting for Peter to do it and Peter was slacking on the job? I don't think so. Jesus was having a last meal with the people he loved before he would suffer the most brutal death. He wanted to honor them. He wanted to show he cared for them. He wanted to leave them an example of how they should act. Jesus is a king. A king, as we know it, is served. He has servants that do the "dirty work." Our king, Jesus, served. Not only did he serve but he did it to the extent that it was the lowliest job. The King of all kings, became a servant to honor those who follow him and to leave an example behind to those who love him. This includes you and me. He left this example for us, not just the disciples. We, too, are to serve one another. We may not wash each other's feet, but Jesus was teaching servant hood, nonetheless.

How does it make you feel knowing Jesus was a servant and a king? Is he any less of a king? Does it actually make him more of a king? Explain.

Look back at verse three. Why did the Holy Spirit direct John to write that? What does it mean in relation to the passage?

Does Jesus expect us to take the lowliest jobs because he did? Or is this just an example?

Name some ways you can become a better servant to those around you.

Day 2 – Read John 13: 6-8a NIV

The passage for today may seem like an odd place to stop, in the middle of a conversation between Jesus and Peter. But I want to focus in on one part of it. You'll remember from yesterday, that Jesus and his disciples are at the last feast they will have together before Jesus goes to the cross. Jesus gets up and begins to wash the disciples' feet, which was customary at the time when a guest enters the house.

Jesus went to Peter to wash his feet. Peter seems a bit perplexed as he asks Jesus if he's going to wash his feet. Peter knows Jesus is king. Peter knows it was his own job to be washing the feet and certainly not one of a king. But, Jesus replies by telling him he doesn't quite understand yet. Understand what? From Peter's perspective, what he knows is that Jesus, the king, is about to wash his feet and that's not acceptable for someone in Jesus's position. Verse 8a Peter very plainly and clearly tells Jesus,

"No."

No to washing his feet. In fact he also says,

"You shall never wash my feet."

At this point Jesus had pointed out that Peter doesn't understand why he's doing this. And it's clear that he doesn't because when you read about Peter, you know he has a heart for Jesus. He believes in Jesus's teachings and he's been following Jesus for a few years now so he's seen the miracles Jesus performed. He's seen him heal and he's seen him give hope and love people. The part I want to emphasize a bit today is Peter's statement in verse 8a,

"You shall never wash my feet."

There is a very strong word in this statement. This word is indefinite. It has no end. This word, "never," is forever or for eternity. Peter, in all his "Peter-ness," thinks he gets it. Thinks he is standing up for Jesus and defending his kingship and Lordship by not letting him wash his feet. But, as Jesus said he doesn't understand. Jesus is coming to Peter like a father to a child. He wants to teach Peter a lesson in a loving way. He wants to share something with Peter and honor him even though he doesn't always get it. Thank God, Jesus is the same way with us. We don't always get it. Jesus is there trying to show us something or teach us something and we try to say, "But wait, Lord"…as if we know what the Lord is doing. We have such a loving God that even as King he is serving. Even as King, he wants to give. Pray to have an open heart to the Lord, that he would show you his heart just as he was showing Peter his character and most of all that you'd let him.

Are there times you can look back and think you were helping Jesus out but you really just didn't get it?

Look up the word "never" in the dictionary, thesaurus and Greek translation and jot down some synonyms.

What was Peter doing here, other than trying to "help out" Jesus and defend his Lordship?

A lot of people seem to like Peter because they can identify with him. Can you identify with him? Are there traits in Peter that you see in yourself?

Day 3- Read John 13: 8b-9 NIV

After yesterday's reaction from Peter to not let the Lord wash his feet, today we will look at Jesus's response. In this section Jesus gives the answer as to why he needs to wash Peter's feet. Jesus is already serving, but even in that he wants to teach Peter as well as all of us.

Peter has insisted that Jesus not wash his feet. But Jesus tells him it's the only way to have a relationship with him. What Peter says next, truly reveals Peter's heart. Peter messes up, he sins, and he even denies Christ three times at one point. But, in the presence of God, learning that the only way to have a relationship with the Lord is to be washed by him, Peter exclaims in verse 9 (NIV),

"Then Lord…not just my feet, but my hands and my head as well."

He doesn't question it. He doesn't ask why he has to be washed by Jesus, he just knows that's what Jesus said. And Peter wants to be a part of Jesus. He loves him. And his exclamation here, shows no hesitancy. Just like when he and Andrew were called out from fishing to follow Jesus and be fishers of men, they didn't hesitate. They jumped right out of the boat and went to Jesus (Matthew 4). Right away, he says, well then wash all of me. In the next verse we'll see why only his feet need to be washed, but for now, let's learn from Peter's excitement, enthusiasm and honest desire to be with the Lord. Jesus wasn't just talking about physically washing Peter (or anyone's) feet. There is a spiritual lesson. Jesus is saying he is the one through whom you get to heaven. We all are dirty from sin. We know that sin cannot enter the kingdom of heaven. So, we need to be washed. The blood shed on the cross cleanses us and wipes away our sin. Yesterday I asked if you can relate to Peter. Today, I'll ask the same in regards to this passage…

Is your reaction to your need to be washed by the blood of Jesus with the same excitement, since of urgency, and full willingness as Peter's was?

We need to understand that Jesus was a servant. He showed the disciples how to live and the thing he did before he went to the cross was to wash their feet. He started with the lowliest, Peter. Jesus seeks out the lowly in this world. One does not have to have it all together to come to him. One doesn't have to be high up in status. Jesus wants all to come as they are to him and let him change their status. Through his servant hood he shows us how to live, he shows honor, he shows love and he teaches about having eternal life with him. All, in this simple act of washing feet.

Sometimes we can be reluctant to have Jesus wash us. Why?

Day 4 – Read John 13: 10-11 NIV

This conversation between Peter and Jesus continues. Peter at first tells Jesus not to wash him. He says this out of ignorance. He doesn't understand that there is a deeper meaning than just physically washing feet. So, then Jesus tells Peter the deeper, spiritual meaning and Peter right away agrees to have Jesus wash him because he wants to be a part of Jesus.

In all of Peter's excitement and urgency to have Jesus wash all of him since he has learned that by having oneself washed by the Lord is the only way to be a part of the Lord, Jesus once again directs and teaches Peter. He tells him that he is already clean, he doesn't need the rest of his body washed. Then Jesus points out that some are not truly clean because he knew Judas was going to betray him.

In these two verses we have again, a practical and cultural application as well as a spiritual application. The practical application is that before these feasts one would take a bath. These feasts were important, they were a big deal. So, people would bathe first to be at their best. By the time they got to the feast only their feet would need to be washed from walking there; their body was clean from their preparation. Jesus tells Peter that he is clean so he will only wash his feet. This could be because Peter bathed before the feast as most would, but I think it could also have a spiritual meaning. Peter knew Jesus. Peter was a follower of Jesus. So, he was saying you have already been washed. His blood was not yet shed, but would be in just hours and Jesus knew what was to come and he knew that blood would cover Peter's sins. Once we accept Christ and make a true confession to have our sin forgiven, nothing can take that away. You can't lose your salvation (1Peter 1:1-5 for the security of our salvation). People stray or lose their closeness to the Lord, but it doesn't mean they've lost their salvation. They need to repent and come back to the Lord. Romans 8:38-39 (NIV) says that nothing can separate us from the love of Christ. Even when you wonder from the Lord, he loves you and calls you back. This is a big day for Peter. He has learned a lot even after being a follower of Christ. Jesus never stops teaching us. He will always continue to bring us closer to him. This conversation between Peter and the Lord probably lasted just a few minutes but there is a lifetime of wisdom from the Lord.

Who do you know today that needs to be washed by the Lord? Add them to your prayer list for this week.

How can you serve this person(s) to show Christ's love?

Day 5- Read John 13: 12-17 NIV

Jesus starts out this last passage for this week's lesson by qualifying who he is. He has finished washing their feet. He reminds them that they call him Teacher and Lord. And he agrees with that saying they should since that's what he is, it's his rightful title. But he says in order to qualify who he is with them so they understand that what he says to them is true, what he says can be trusted. He gives them instruction and tells them that they should also wash each other's feet because that's the example he left for them. He again qualifies this statement by saying in verse 16 (NIV),

> "I tell you the truth, no servant is greater than his master, nor
> messenger greater than the one who sent him."

Jesus is their master. If washing feet wasn't too low for him, then they ought to wash each other's feet as well. Jesus was willing to do whatever it took to teach them how to live, even becoming a servant. A foot washer was the lowest job. Jesus, even in all his glory, *became a foot washer to the foot washer!* He lowered himself even more than any of the disciples could have lowered themselves. Just as he did on the cross. Perhaps this makes him even more glorious. This is what makes him the only true teacher. He lead by example and taught them by showing them. He was never just on his high throne giving orders. He came to earth, lived fully human, experienced temptations that humans experience. Why? Ultimately because he loves you and me. He is our savior who knows what it's like to walk in our shoes, he is sympathetic and empathetic. Only he is much more. He knows what it's like to walk in our shoes, but we will never know what it's like to walk in his shoes. He carried our burden so we wouldn't have to. Such an amazing God. One that I want to know, and it starts with being a servant.

Look at verse 17 again. What is our responsibility now that he has taught these things?

What will happen if we obey according to verse 17?

What's the greatest lesson or price of information you can take away from this week?

This Week's Extra Tid-Bits:

"We have all been called to be foot-washers". – R. Alan Woods

"The only way Jesus can be our King is if we allow him to be our servant" — Stuart Greaves

This Week's Prayers:

_____
_____
_____
_____
_____
_____
_____
_____
_____
_____
_____
_____
_____

This Week's Praises and Thanksgiving:

_____
_____
_____
_____
_____
_____
_____
_____
_____
_____
_____
_____
_____
_____

Lesson 8 (Week 8)

Accepting without Accepting

Arguably, one of the greatest longings we have on this earth is to be accepted. This is a universal desire. Everyone wants to be accepted. People don't want to put on a facade to gain people's acceptance, but they do. Where does this longing come from? Even the most "successful" people on this earth seem to be longing for something. A person does well at their job, is raising a wonderful family, perhaps volunteers, runs marathons, and donates to charity, why would this person be longing to be accepted? This kind of person sounds like they have it all. Good job, family, good health…what is it in our being makes us to long for acceptance? We'll answer that question this week as well look at accepting people without accepting their sin.

Day 1- Read Genesis 3 NIV

Longing comes from a void. That's the only reason it exists in the first place. If there weren't something to fill, there wouldn't be a need to fill it. This void at its deepest point, at its root is the need for Jesus. As a human race, we once had fellowship with the Lord. In Genesis, in the Garden of Eden, Adam and Eve talked with God and walked with God. There is some debate in the theological world as to whether this was God physically walking or his presence was there by spirit, either way, they were there in fellowship with God (Genesis 3:8a and 9). Adam and Eve had all they needed and were even put in leadership over all the animals. But, when you read chapter 3 in its entirety you see the complete account of how fellowship turned to distrust and separation. After Adam and Eve sinned, there was a separation between God and all of mankind because we are the descendants of Adam and Eve. Thus, our void began. We have a longing to be accepted because of a void that was created when Adam and Eve no longer had fellowship with God.

Our longing comes out in different forms. In our day and age, it may be wanting acceptance from peers. It may be wanting acceptance from parents, teachers, or coaches. We want to know we are loved and accepted so this reveals itself in many ways. But, the origin was established a long time ago with our original parents and passed down to every generation. That's the very core of its origins, the deepest root of the longing comes from that separation.

In Genesis 3, who/what enticed Adam and Eve to sin?

How was this accomplished?

Has the enemy's tactics changed?

What do you long for?

Day 2 – Read Romans 15:7

Yesterday's lesson was one of learning the source of our desire to be accepted. We learned that this deep longing that everyone has at some point, if not always, originates from the Garden of Eden. It's because there is a separation between God and man.

The good news is that it doesn't have to be that way anymore. God made a way to bring man back into fellowship with himself. And that was done through the death and resurrection of Jesus. Because of this *you are accepted!* You don't have to try to be loved. You don't have to live your life in an outlandish way, you don't have to draw attention to yourself, especially in a negative way to be noticed. God notices you. God loves you. God accepts you. Romans 15:7 (NIV) says,

"Accept one another, then, just as Christ accepted you, in order to bring praise to God."

Right in the middle of the verse it says you are accepted! You can stop trying. Give yourself a break. Let's clarify what it does not say. It doesn't say you are accepted once you do x, y, z. It does not say you are accepted once you make $x per year. It does not say you are accepted once you buy all the latest trends in clothes. This verse states that you already have been accepted. It's done. There's nothing to add to try to earn it or gain it.

It's important to look at whose standard are we going by when trying to gain acceptance. Are we going by the government's standard? Are we going by the coach's standards? God's standard is the ultimate one. It's ok to please your coaches, parents, spouse or even your pastor. We are to try our best in all we do. But, God's standard is the only one that counts. He is the one we need to look to when having a guideline for our life. He is the one with authority. What gives him that authority? He's the creator. He's the Father. He's the Savior and he's the Judge. So, while it is ok to do your best and please others in this world and want to be accepted by them, remember that God is the ultimate one and whom we should want to be accepted by. And, according to Romans 15:7 you are already accepted!

Here's a list of verses dealing with God's authority. Each one talks about his authority in different ways. Read each one and jot down the main way God is in authority for that verse.

Matthew 28:18

Colossians 1:18

Ephesians 2:10

Are there other verses that show God's authority? List them here with a brief description of his authority.

Besides Romans 15:7, what other verses show you are accepted by the Father?

Day 3-Read Romans 15:7 NIV

So far we've looked at that everyone longs to be accepted and we've seen that you are accepted. Both those facts deal with the person as a person, as a human being, as a creation of the Lord, you have been accepted. Today we'll look at what happens when a person is doing wrong. Are we supposed to accept everyone even when they live a life contrary to God? Is this person still accepted by God?

There is no doubt, in this world, everyone who is a believer knows people who aren't. Every believer knows someone, many people who claim they don't believe in God, don't have faith or have faith in something that is demonic and presents false teaching. We all know someone, if not multiple people who don't care about faith but just want to live a lifestyle according to their terms whether it's sinful or not. This is the nature of a fallen world. This is the nature of men (this is a general term) being stuck in or blinded to sin. Are we supposed to love them anyway? Are we supposed to turn our nose to them because they don't live according to God's will?

There's two parts to this. <u>First</u> – God loves every single person that has ever walked this earth and ever will. Every person since Adam and Eve is a creation by God. Each person was fashioned in the womb of their mother just the way God intended (Psalms 139:14 NIV). So, there shouldn't ever be a question as to whether or not God loves someone. John 3:16 (NIV) says that when he came to this world to die on the cross he did it for *all* to have everlasting life. He didn't do it for some. He did it for *all*. He loves everyone, even when they are in sin and living contrary to his will. <u>Second</u> – there is a difference in loving someone and not loving their lifestyle or attitude. I love my children unconditionally. But, every parent knows my kids and your kids will do things wrong, will sin, will have times of not listening to you as the parent. I still love my kids. I have people close to me I know live contrary to God's will and design but I love them. And always will. I don't like their choices, but I love them. I still talk to them, I still associate with them and still love being around them. It is possible to love someone and not their actions, their lifestyle, their attitude, the foul language they use, etc. So it is with God. He loved us while we were sinners, before we came to know him and have our sin forgiven (Romans 5:8). He's the Father. He loves everyone because they are his creation. Even Jesus walked, talked, ate with and associated with sinners. But that does not mean he condoned their actions! It does not mean he said it's ok to live however one wants. One common excuse amongst non-believers is that the Bible is full of things contrary to how God says we should live therefore because of all the "contradictions" it is untrustworthy and made up. The answer to that is simply God did not condone everything in the Bible! He did condone that the authors write about it for our instruction as well as our history. But, the people in the Bible were real people who live daily lives just like you and I do. They were sinners just like you and me. The Bible is an account of the history of the world in its entirety, the beginning all the way to the end (which includes the future from our present time). It is reporting the facts. There was sin back in those days, too. So, you'll see it in the accounts of the people's lives back then. It is not a contradiction to say what really happened but then to say what should happen. That is simply revealing sin and offering correction. So, it is with people we know that are living outside God's will. We love them, but we do not condone their actions. We looked at Romans 15:7 (NIV) yesterday but we mainly discussed the middle part that says you are accepted. Look at the beginning of the verse. It's a command. What are we to do? It says,

"Accept one another."

This is not an option. It doesn't beg us to accept each other. It doesn't say if you want to or feel like it. It very poignantly says,

"Accept one another."

This is in a portion of scripture when Paul is speaking about the Jews and gentiles. It is talking about those of faith and those not of faith. So, very clearly we see that we are to accept one another even those that may live contrary to the Lord's will. We aren't, however, supposed to accept the sin. Jesus taught the people, not so they could stay in their sin, but so they could recognize it and turn from it. Jesus did not condone sin. What would that make the cross? If by telling us to accept people Jesus is also saying to let them be in their sin, then the cross is negated. It is pointless. Jesus died on the cross to take away sin. Sin needs to go. That's why he gave up his life – to pay our price of sin. So, clearly Jesus cared for people, he interacted with people but he did not approve of their sin and taught that they should repent. This is our attitude towards the unbelievers in our life, too. We are to love them and pray for them. We are not to disown them or treat them as "less than." We are to love them, but call sin for what it is and point people to the truth.

Look up John 13:35. What does it say and how does it relate to today's lesson?

What is our ultimate goal as Christians? How does John 13:35 relate?

Do you have a hard time accepting or showing someone love who is in sin? How can you love them better?

Day 4 – Read 2 Timothy 2:24-26 NIV

Now that we've established we need to love one another regardless, we can talk about how to do so. How to handle the sin. How do we love someone and associate with them when we know they are living contrary to God's will.

This passage in 2 Timothy is actually instruction for us about how to conduct ourselves as Christians. If we follow these things God can work through us to change the lives of non-believers. Yesterday we talked at length about accepting one another without accepting the sin. Today, we talk about how to have a good attitude and show non-believers and those in sin how to have hope and know the Lord.

Verse 24 gives us four things to do. List those four things here:

1.
2.
3.
4.

I don't know about you, but for me it's so easy to get worked up or raise my voice when discussing the things of God to a non-believer. If one is not careful this kind of thing can lead to an argument and can come across as hateful to the other person. So we are to be kind and calm. We're also to be ready to teach. We should know the word. We should know what the Lord says and if we have the opportunity be able to open the Bible and present the scripture to someone. The fourth thing it says we are to do is not be resentful. People aren't always going to immediately agree with us. People aren't always going to want to hear what you have to say about the Lord. Don't take it personal and don't become bitter or resentful toward that person. Have patience and pray.

The first part of verse 25 gives another instruction. What does it say to do?

And how does it say to do it?

The Lord is so kind and gentle with everyone. He has been with you and me or we wouldn't even be learning about him. So, we too, are to be gentle with people.

Finally, the last part of verse 25 and all of verse 26 says why we are to conduct ourselves this way. Fill in the blanks to complete these two verses. I say am using the NIV but you should still be able to get it with another version.

"...in the _____ that God will grant them _____
leading them to a knowledge of _____, and that they will come to
their _____ and _____ from the trap of the devil, who has
taken them _____ to do his will."

Is there anything in verse 24 you feel you don't do? Add it to your prayer list and ask God to give you this ability. Jot it down here.

Yesterday, I asked what our ultimate goal as Christians is and how John 13:35 relates. Today, look at 2 Tim. 2:25b-26 and answer the same question. What is our ultimate goal as a Christian?

Day 5- Read Romans 15:7 NIV

This week may have provoked different emotions in some of you. Accepting people can be a controversial topic. Unfortunately, we still live in a world with much prejudice, bias and hatred. Even in the year I write this, 2014, we think of these things as happening a long time ago, but if you look around in the world they are still very prevalent. In some ways, such as against Christianity and the things of God it has gotten worse. Spiritually speaking, there are those that tend to turn their back on sinners, there are those who tend to turn their nose up at those who struggle or live contrary to God. This week was about exposing a real need. One that everyone has. We all want/need to be accepted because of the separation that took place in Genesis. As stated on day one, at the beginning of this lesson, the good news is God made a way to restore us to him and you are already accepted. I hope that as you conclude this lesson you can be more aware of those around you. I want to be very clear that I am not suggesting we don't call sin, sin. I do suggest we call sin, sin. In fact, we've gotten a little too "loosy goosy." We should be calling out sin for what it is. But, what is just as important is that we are loving people. And in calling out sin, we show people love, gentleness and point them to Jesus. If God has accepted me, a sinner, I too, can accept the sinner. God didn't accept my sin as acceptable. He brought me to repentance and forgiveness, but he loved me enough to do that. We, too, need to be loving people enough to show them the truth of their sin, and point them to Christ so he can bring them to repentance. Our job is to love and point people in the right direction. God's job is to bring them to repentance and begin a work in them. Review Romans 15:7 (NIV) one more time. You'll notice that the end says,

"…in order to bring praise to God."

We are to accept people, just as Christ accepted us because it will bring him glory and praise. How has this lesson impacted you this week?

Are there ways you can ask God to make you more accepting of people while not condoning their sin?

Who can you pray for that God would bring to repentance in order to show them the truth (2 Tim. 2:25-26)

This Week's Extra tid-bits:

Romans 14:1 "As for the one who is weak in faith, welcome him, but not to quarrel over opinions."

This Week's Prayers:

_____
_____
_____
_____
_____
_____
_____
_____
_____
_____
_____
_____
_____
_____
_____
_____

This Week's Praises and Thanksgiving:

_____
_____
_____
_____
_____
_____
_____
_____
_____
_____
_____
_____
_____
_____
_____

Lesson 9 (week 9)

Patience: It's a Virtue

This week is all about timing and patience. You will see that God's time of getting things done is not always the time in which we want something done. But, you will also see that his is best; from the biggest down to the smallest detail in your life.

Day 1 – Read 2 Peter 3:8 NIV

Let's start with context. In chapter 3 of 2 Peter, Peter is writing to believers as a reminder and an encouragement. He tells them to take heart and remember that scoffers are going to criticize and mock the Lord for his promises. And because of this they will point fingers and accuse God of not keeping his promises. The promise they are referring to is that of the second coming of Jesus. Since it hadn't happened yet, even in that day they were scoffing at the believers saying things like in verse 4 (NIV),

"Where is this coming he promised?"

But, in verse 8 we are reminded that God's timing is not our own. Our timing is quite different. We typically expect results or answers right away, sometimes instantly. I know I've caught myself frustrated at my computer when a page from the internet takes a few seconds to load. A few seconds! Because it didn't load instantly I say it's too slow. We've grown acustom to this kind of time. Even back when Peter was writing this, scoffers were impatient. Because a promise hadn't happened yet, they were more than willing to use that as a reason as to why it wasn't going to happen and justify their unbelief. Here we are 2,014 years after Christ was born and the second coming hasn't happened yet. Does that mean it won't? Does that mean God is a liar? Or is our timing just not God's?

I suggest it's the latter. Our timing is not God's. And thankfully so, because his timing is perfect. Ours isn't. We need to be patient. At the beginning of verse 8 Peter says not to forget this. He tells us to *not* forget because the Holy Spirit who is directing him on what to write knows we *will* forget. The Holy Spirit knows we will become impatient and impatience can start the ball rolling for doubt. He says,

"But do not forget this one thing, dear friends: With the Lord a day is
like a thousand years, and a thousand years are like a day."

Some translations use the word "as" instead of "like." It doesn't matter which is used. Either one is a similie and similies are used to compare two things. So it is not saying one day *is* a thousand years and a thousand years *is* one day. It's a comparison to show us that to God time doesn't matter; it's not the same to him as it is to us. He is outside of time. When the Lord promises something you can count on it. He promised it then, it's still a promise now. To him, there's no change. Making a promise two thousand years ago or even more, is the same as making a promise yesterday or today to the Lord. That's hard for us to understand sometimes because one thousand or two thousand years is a long time when our lives are a mere eighty, maybe ninety years on this earth at best. But to God, and the way we need to remember it, is it's all the same. It doesn't matter how long it's been in earthly time. He will keep his promise. This is true for all his promises not just that of the second coming.

Why do think it's so hard for us to be patient?

Have you caught yourself wondering is God's promises will ever be fullfilled?

What's one question you have, if any, about God's time verses our time? Do you have any questions about Peter's statement in verse 8 regarding a thousand years verses one day? If so, jot it down here and discuss in your group. If doing this individually, take some time to research it online or through commentaries.

Day 2 – Read 2 Peter 3:9 NIV

Yesterday we looked at God's timing compared to our timing. We saw that they are different and that God's timing is perfect and his concept of time is different than ours in that to him it's one big picture regardless of how long something takes to us on earth. Today, in verse 9, we will see why God waits to fulfill his promise.

Right off, Peter says God is not slow. At least the way we may understand it. We have to remember this is God the creator. He created all things. He's the one who separated the day from the night. If anyone understands time and its passage it's the one who created it. So Peter says definitively, God is not slow. You may have been waiting for that better job or promotion but it hasn't come yet, despite all your applications and resumes sent out. You may have been waiting to meet someone and get married again, or for the first time and now here you are in your thirties, forties, or older and never been married. Maybe you've been waiting to be healed. Maybe you've been praying for someone to know the Lord for years but they still don't. There are a myriad of possibilities that we feel are taking too long. If we are giving these things to the Lord in prayer and trusting him, then they aren't taking too long. I know it's so hard for us to believe that. But, when we believe that it's because we are thinking in our own time. We forget God's time. Peter says he is not slow. And he will fulfill his perfect will in anyone who is following him.

Remember Peter is talking specifically about the promise of the Second Coming, though God is not slow in anything. The reason he delays his coming is because he loves each and every person. He does not want any to die. We will all die on earth, but he is talking about eternal death. After one dies on this earth, anyone who doesn't know the Lord spends eternity in hell. The Lord is our creator, he doesn't want his creation, his beloved in an eternal separation from him. So, he waits. He waits on everyone to have a chance to accept him. It's his will that all would repent and spend eternity with him. We all know people that need the Lord. We all know people that don't know him. Are we praying for them? Are we witnessing to them? Are we being kind to them? You'll recall last week's lesson on acceptance. Are we loving on people in sin? We are not to love the sin, we are not to accept the sin. We are to call out the sin. But we are to love people. We are to lovingly show them Christ. We all come from a sinful background, that's why we all need a savior. So, not only is the Lord patiently waiting for more to come to him, but we too, need to be patient while we love and care for people so we can let the Holy Spirit minister to them.

What are some things in your life that you need to be patient with?

Are there things you feel like you've had to wait so long for and still hasn't come to fruition? Write them down and commit them to your prayer list this week. If you're in a group share if you'd like.

Look up and write down some scriptures about God's patience.

Look up and write down some scriptures about our patience. What does God say about us having patience?

Give an example of someone in the Bible who had to wait a long time to see a promise from God fulfilled.

Day 3 – Read 2 Peter 3:10 NIV

The Lord, as we've seen, has great patience. His patience is long. And he does it because his will is for everyone to know him. Does that mean it will go on forever? Does it mean there is no end?

Verse 10 and several places in the Bible, suggest that God's patience will not last forever. There will be an end to it. There will be a day when the Lord says that's enough. Just as a father has to stop his children from fighting when it gets to be too much, so our Father will stop all evil and wrong doing and his patience will be no more. As great as his patience is, it would not be right if it lasted forever. Would it be right for a father to let his children fight out of anger even to the point of someone getting hurt, breaking bones, knocking out teeth and so on? That father would stop it. And rightfully so, because the father's job is to protect his children and teach them how to get along and settle arguments when they aren't getting along. So it is with God. He has us in this world, we go through trials, we go through tough times, and it's all to teach us and grow us. But, when it gets to a certain point the Lord will say enough and pull his children out of the fight so to speak.

Verse 10 (NIV) says,

"But, the day of the Lord will come like a thief."

A thief is not expected though you can prepare for a thief. One may have an alarm system wired in their house or a big, loud, scary dog. One might even have fire arms as a protection. These things would prepare you for the thief, but you still wouldn't know when one was coming. The Lord says this is how the day of the Lord will be. We can and should be prepared, in our relationship with Christ, but we do not know when it will take place.

If the Lord's patience had no ending, what would happen?

Why then, must the Lord's patience come to an end (there are several reasons)?

What other scriptures can you think of that mirrors 2 Peter 3:10? Search for some if you can't think of any.

Day 4 – Read Matthew 18:21-35 NIV

We've seen that God has tremendous patience but that it will not last forever. We've seen that we should have patience as well, to wait for his plan to be fulfilled but also for other people. We'll talk about two points to add to this topic of patience today. The first is a question. God's patience has an end so should ours? Is there ever a time we can throw the towel in and not be patient with someone? The second is forgiveness. Forgiveness and patience can often go hand in hand. Sometimes you need to have patience with someone because they haven't reach a certain point yet, they are learning at their own pace or God hasn't brought them there yet. Other times we need to have patience with people because we must keep forgiving them.

In Matthew, Jesus gives a parable about an unmerciful servant when Peter asks him how many times one should forgive another. In the parable Jesus says we should forgive seventy times seven. Some versions may say seventy and some may say seventy-seven. In this explanation I will use seven times seventy. This number does not mean literally, 490 times (seven times seventy). It shows an unending forgiveness which goes hand in hand with patience. When we forgive someone we have to be patient with them and their mistake. In the parable a man cannot repay his debt. Therefore he, his family and all he had were going to be sold. He begged for forgiveness and his master showed it to him, letting him go. He then, saw a fellow servant that owned him money. He forcefully demanded the money back. The second servant asked for forgiveness as he could not pay his debt either. The first servant had him put in jail and did not forgive him. Word got around to the master and he was greatly disappointed. The first servant had been shown mercy and forgiveness but he did not show it in return.

Our Father in heaven has forgiven us many times, daily for me. If a perfect God, who has every right not to forgive since we disobeyed in the Garden, forgives, all the more should we. We might call this concept, "paying it forward." Whatever the name, in answering our original question, our forgiveness and patience should not end. There will be a time when God's does, but he is the Judge as much as he is the Forgiver. He has the right to do so. We, do not. We are the ones that have been forgiven. Why wouldn't we then, forgive?

** Note to clarify: *Since we are not to have an end to our forgiveness or patience, it does not mean that there isn't ever a time when we move on. There may be a time when someone becomes toxic to be around. Sure, we should have patience with that person but at some point if they are corrupting you or your family having patience and forgiving them doesn't mean you have to be around them. In this case, continue to pray for them, be kind to them, love them even if it's at a distance, but fulfill your duty to have a Godly home and protect your marriage, your children, other relationships, or whatever it may be that is involved.*

Who is the master like in this parable?

Who is the servant like in this parable?

What was the outcome for the first servant who was forgiven but did not show forgiveness?

What is the warning from Jesus at the end of the parable?

So, what are we to do?

Day 5 – Read 2 Peter 3:15a NIV

Today we will wrap up the lesson on patience with the first half of this verse. Simply put, it says,

"Bear in mind, that our Lord's patience means salvation…"

Some synonyms for the phrase "bear in mind" include: be mindful, take into consideration or take into account. So, as we end this week's lesson be mindful of God's patience. Remember it. Beyond this week when things in your life seem to be moving slow or when you don't know why things haven't happened yet, remember that God is not slow, his timing is perfect and he will fulfill His promises. When it comes to scoffers, family members, the media, non-believers wanting to accuse, or your own doubts creep in, take into consideration, remember what the Lord's patience means and why his patience is so great. Verse 15 (NIV) says the Lord's patience means salvation. Just remember he is waiting for all who will come to know him, to come. He is waiting so none should be left behind. He is waiting because of his unconditional love. It was that love that brought him to the cross and he will see it through until every last person accepts him that will accept him. We know not everyone will. But he is faithful to give everyone the opportunity.

Remember also, that we are to have patience and forgiveness for others. In the difficult times of being patient with someone, ask God to help you. Love them and pray for them.

This week we have looked at several points about patience, list five of them (there are many more):

1.
2.
3.
4.
5.

This Week's Extra Tid-bit

"A patient man has great understanding…" Proverbs 14:29

This Week's Prayers:

_____
_____
_____
_____
_____
_____
_____
_____
_____
_____
_____
_____
_____
_____
_____
_____

This Week's Praises and Thanksgiving:

_____
_____
_____
_____
_____
_____
_____
_____
_____
_____
_____
_____
_____
_____
_____
_____
_____

Lesson 10 (Week 10)

Rest in Him

Have you ever just sat in a quiet room and did nothing for the purpose of being still? Have you ever sat outside on a spring or summer evening at night when it's quiet? If you live in the country or outskirts of town you can probably hear the crickets, maybe some frogs. How do you feel when you take time to quiet yourself? Relaxed? Refreshed? Maybe you've never done this. This week we will discover why it's so important to your growth in the Lord to take time to be still.

Day 1 – Read Psalm 46:1-3 NIV

Once you've read today's verses notice the contrast between verse 1 and verses 2 and 3. It starts with verse 1 by telling us where our help comes from. Then, verses 2 and 3 talk about why we need that help. Verse 1 tells us that,

> "God is our refuge and strength, an ever-present help in trouble."

When there is trouble in our life, God is the one to go to. According to this scripture he is three things to us just in this verse. First, he is our refuge. Look up and write the definition of refuge here:

One possible definition is "being safe from pursuit." If you wrote down a different definition, that's ok, there's more than one correct way of stating the meaning. The Lord is our refuge. He is the safe place when we are being pursued. When you are going through trials, sickness, death of a loved one, or you just feel the enemy is really throwing you some attacks, know and come to God as your safe place, as your shelter, as your refuge. The second characteristic this verse says God is to us is our strength. When we are weak, whether it be physically or by way of temptation, God is our strength. He steps in for us and carries us. Just as the old poem, "Footprints" suggests. In this poem, the author's dream reveals only one set of footprints in the sand during difficult times. It is then realized that the one set of footprints shows Christ carrying us during those times. He never leaves us or abandons us, rather picks us up and carries through times in which we need him most. The third characteristic of God to us in times of trouble in the ever-present help. He doesn't just show up to help whenever he has time. He doesn't just run to our aid whenever he finds it convenient. These are not the ways of our Lord. It says he is ever-present. Always there. Always present. Always available. You call on him and he will be there.

Now that we've established three characteristics of God in times of trouble, what trouble are we talking about. If a student cheats on a test and receives a failing grade as a result then gets in trouble at home, is that what it's talking about? Well, I would suggest that in a scenario like this the student certainly should take it to God and ask forgiveness and to be his strength to not cheat again, but in this particular part of scripture, we see in verses 2 and 3 that it's specially talking about natural disasters. He is our refuge, strength and ever-present help certainly in natural disasters but also in our character, our behavior and our decisions. Take whatever gives you trouble or whatever trial you have and let God be those three comforts to you – refuge, strength and help.

Back to the beginning of this lesson. I asked you to notice the order of the verses. Verse 1 starts with the reassurance of who God is to us and then it talks about why we need his reassurance and from what.

Why might he state it in this order? Why not state the trouble first and then say, "But, God is our refuge…"

What are two things happening to the earth in verses 2-3?

At the beginning of verse 2 what are we to do?

What are the three characteristics of God to us in this passage?

Day 2 – Read Psalm 46:10 NIV

This verse is the focus of this week's lesson, try memorizing it this week

After yesterday's lesson you're probably wondering how that had anything to do with being still as I said this week would be about at the introduction of the lesson. Well, yesterday was just setting the stage. We talked about having trouble. We can have all kinds of trouble in our life; from natural things of this earth to trials within our lives and even trials within ourselves personally. So we briefly talked about those and God's characteristics in times of trouble. Today, we will dial in on one thing – the theme of this week.

This is in the same chapter as what we talked about yesterday in regards to trouble, disaster and God being our refuge, strength and help. It's still on the same topic and a continuation. That was all a precursor as to why we need to be still. So, keep all that mind as we go about the rest of the week's lesson.

Being still, quieting oneself is not an easy thing to do. We lead busy lives. We have children that need to get places such as practice or lessons and school. We need to get to a meeting for work or PTA. We need to run errands and pay bills all the while the house is mounting up with dishes and laundry. Psalm 46:10 (NIV) tells us an important truth that while it is a common verse often quoted it doesn't get remembered or practiced as much as it should.

"Be still, and know that I am God."

The first thing said is an instruction. It says,

"Be still."

Very straight forward. Often when we hear the word "still" or "be still" we think of movement. We think we shouldn't have any movement, physically. We should keep our body from moving. That is part of it. But, I'm going to suggest the part that we often lack is that of the mind. Grab a dictionary or do a search online for the word "still." What do you come up with for the definition? Write it here:

111

Did you find that part of the definition is about being still with one's mind and not just the physical body? One definition I found online, that really shows the importance of being still is, "deep silence and calm." This clearly shows that when we are still we should be in silence. It's not just a physical, not moving of the body.

What adjective is before silence?

What does this mean? How should you be in silence?

Not only are we talking about silence but we are also talking about calm according to the definition. To be clam means to be relaxed, tranquil, unflustered. This is not easy to achieve. With our busy lives as I described earlier it's very easy to never really be still according to these definitions. Yet, God calls us to do this. His words, very clearly say,

"Be still."

He is not wanting us to just quit everything and do nothing in the name of being still. It's about context and balance. God also calls us to be about his business. God created the world in six days then rested. Why? Because he knew we would need rest. He knew we would need time to refresh and be still. By God's own model we can see that there is a place for work, but we need to be sure that once in a while we are to rest and be still.

Have you ever truly been still before the Lord now that we've looked at these definitions?

Knowing these meanings of "still" or "be still" what are some ways/times you can commit to being still for a time?

Search the scriptures. What other verses do you find that speak about being still. List any here with a brief description.

Day 3 – Read Psalm 46:10 NIV, Psalm 100:3 NIV

Calming oneself, being quiet, silent, unflustered, relaxed, these are all descriptions of being still. Yesterday we talked about these and the deeper meaning to being still. Of the verse Psalm 46:10 we only touched on the first two words, "Be still." It has such importance, especially in our fast paced world that we need to spend time learning about it and putting it into practice. But, today we will look at the rest of the verse as well as Psalm 100:3 (NIV). This portion of scripture is also important. It says,

> "…and know that I am God."

You'll remember from yesterday that this is an instruction on what we are to do. There are two instructions. The first is to be still, the second it to know that God is God. These two instructions are tied together with the word, "and." Because of this we know they go together. "And" is a word that connects phrases or clauses. So we can be still all we want and truly grasp what it means to be still but if we do not know that God is God and let him be God then what good is being still? Yes, it may still have physical benefits to a person. It's good physically to be still once in a while in a manner of rest so we don't get run down and possibly even get sick from exhaustion. But, since we looked at the definitions yesterday we know that that is only the half of being still. The mind is the other half. We need to quiet our mind so that we can refocus it on what's really important. It allows us to know that God is God. This sounds like a statement so simple that it also seems pointless to say. Of course God is God. But, often we don't live like it. We live like we are God. We want to take control of our lives. We want to make decisions without taking it to God first and asking for his direction. We will put things before God making them idols in our life. So, it is easy to say God is God and say we *know* that God is God, but do we really?

Psalm 100:3 (NIV) says,

> "Know that the Lord is God. It is He who made us, and we are
> his; we are his people, the sheep of his pasture."

Again, this verse just like Psalm 46:10 (NIV) says,

> "know…"

It doesn't just say God is God or the Lord is God. It says,

> "<u>Know</u> that the Lord is God."

Why does the Lord use the word "know?" What are your thoughts? Jot it down here:

The Lord knows while we may not forget it on an intellectual level, we most likely will forget it on an experiential level; how we live it out. So, he reminds us that we are to know that the Lord is God in a way that we show it. In knowing this we can truly let him control our lives and we can do it without fear. When we know who God is it frees us because we know that he is in control and has way better decision making power than we do. So, he can guide our lives in a much more productive and righteous way than we can.

Since the two instructions are connected in chapter 46 verse 10 with the word *"and"* we know they go together. We need to be still *and* know he is God. This allows us to hear the Lord in the times of quietness, in times of stillness, in times of deep silence and calmness. These are often the times we can hear him speaking to us, directing us, guiding us. Even if there's times in the stillness that we don't hear him speaking to us we are still sitting in his presence. We are still being refreshed by spending time with him.

What does the phrase *the Lord is God* mean to you?

Recall from memory and/or search the scriptures for someone in the Bible who knew what it meant to be still in the Lord? How did this person be still in the Lord? How did he/she *know* that the Lord is God? Give a synopsis.

There's a certain element of comfort in knowing the Lord is God. How does this comfort you?

Day 4 – Read Psalm 100:4-5 NIV

This week, so far has been one of taking two seemingly simple concepts, "be still" and "know that the Lord is God," and analyzing them, digging deeper into means and applications. Now that we have studied what those instructions are in a deeper way, there is also a responsibility we have and response that we are to have in light of this knowledge.

When the Lord does speak to us in times of stillness we then have a responsibility to respond. We have a duty to act on what he told us if it were a directive word. We also have a responsibility in what we do with the information of knowing we need to be still and know he is God. We may say we know it, but until we act on it and put these things into practice, we are not obeying God.

We have a responsibility to live out this knowledge. We are to live like we believe this knowledge. Again, that is a simple statement. One might say, "Of course, I believe God is God. I'm a Christian." But, so often it's not just what we say, it's what others see. So, we need to be living a life that actually shows that we know God is God. This will come out in our attitude, the words we use when we speak, and how we treat others. It will also be known in how we approach a difficult situation. Are we freaking out? Or are we letting God be God, by being still in his presence and understanding that he is in control?

Psalm 101:2 (NIV) says,

> "I will be careful to lead a blameless life…"

How does leading a blameless life contribute to living out our responsibility to know the Lord is God?

In Psalm 100:4-5 what should our response (in terms of attitude) be to that of verse 3, knowing the Lord is God, knowing that he is the one that made us.

Day 5 – Read Psalm 46:1-3, 10 NIV, Psalm 100:3-5 NIV

God is our _____ and strength. Because of this I can be reassured that whenever I am going through a tough time he will be my _____ - _____
_____

Two ways I can I can alleviate and abolish altogether my fears and anxieties in times of trouble or with the busyness of this world is to _____ _____ and _____ that the _____ is _____. To be still means (pick three attributes, there's many more) to be _____, _____, _____. When I am still it should not just be my body but also my _____. Being still allows me to hear from God. It allows me to clear my mind so there are no distractions. Even if I don't hear from God specially, I am still in his _____. It is important to know the Lord is God because often times we say we know it but our lives show a different belief. My life may show that _____ or _____
is more important. So if I'm not consciously aware or live like the Lord is God I may mislead people or push them away from the Lord. It is also important to know the Lord is _____ because it can be _____ . Knowing he is God takes the pressure off me. I am not in control. My life needs to be one that shows I know God is in control. This is accomplished through my _____ and actions. "Be still and know that I am God" is a (n) _____ from God's word. He tells us this is what we are to do. So, if I don't do it, I am not obeying God.

Lord, please help me to grow in you. Help me to make times in which I can be still and sit in your presence so that I will grow. It is in these times that I can hear you intimately. It's in these times that it's just my Father and me. Help me to know that you are God. This means I need to let you be God in my life. I take comfort in knowing you know best and are in control. I do not have to go through trials alone. I pray you would give me strength to go deeper with you. I want to *know* you are God. In Jesus name, Amen.

This Week's Extra Tid-Bit:

Listen to "Strong Tower" by Kutless and/or Newsboys

"Read "Footprints in the Sand" by Mary Stevenson

This Week's Prayers:

_____
_____
_____
_____
_____
_____
_____
_____
_____
_____
_____
_____

This Week's Praises and Thanksgiving:

_____
_____
_____
_____
_____
_____
_____
_____
_____
_____
_____
_____

Lesson 11 (Week 11)

God Became Flesh and Blood because You are Flesh and Blood

This week we will look at God's qualifications for being a personal God. He's not a removed or distant God. He is very much active in our lives and he's qualified to do so; not just because he is God, but because he also, was human.

Day 1 – Read Hebrews 2:10-11 NIV

This section of verses talks about family. I have heard numerous times that God is real, he exists, but he's distant. He is not involved in our lives, it is all up to us to run the show on earth. The Bible suggests otherwise. He is very personable. In fact, when one accepts Jesus he does so individually. It's a personal decision one must make to invite the Lord into their life. Starting in verse 10 (NIV) God says,

> "…it was fitting…"

It was fitting or right that Jesus would die on the cross. It wasn't fitting because God has no heart and cast Jesus to death without any regard to him. It's quite the opposite. God cares for and loves each and every one of us, we are his creation, and we are his people. He knew that would be the only way to restore the relationship with his beloved people back to himself. He had every person that would ever live, literally, in mind when he sent his son. Many of those insurmountable number of people would come to know him because of Jesus's death. So, the Lord says,

> "…it was fitting."

Verse 11 gets more in depth about family. God is holy. We, on our own are not. However, with God we are made holy. Holy does not mean perfect. Holy does not mean one who doesn't sin (though those are characteristics of God). I think these are often the descriptions people think of when they hear the word "holy." It isn't so. Holy actually means "set apart." According to online searches, it means, "Dedicated or consecrated to God or a religious purpose" (probably the only time you'll see the word "religious" in this book, as our relationship with Jesus is not a religion it is knowing him; a relationship). It simply means dedicated to…So when God makes us holy he isn't making us perfect. He isn't making us sinless. As long as we are on this earth in this earthly body, we will sin. God forgives us, but we will never be perfect here. What he does do, though, is set us apart, when we accept him and washes us clean, we are dedicating ourselves to him and he is setting us apart. We are no longer about the purposes of the world. We are for the purposes of God. Still in verse 11 (NIV) we read,

> "Both the One who makes men holy and those who are made holy are of the same family."

So, we've established that God is the holy one and we are those made holy by him. We are family. We are of the same unit. Maybe there's been times when you have felt distant in your own family, or like you are different than them, or maybe there's family members you just don't know. You've never been close to them or maybe you once were and had a falling out.

Jesus calls us family and the word says he's not ashamed. In fact, he delights in it. He loves us more than we will ever understand. He knows our every quirk, what makes our personality different, silly, serious, adventurous or mysterious to others, he knows. He created you. By the way, he makes no mistakes. So the way you are in your personality, your talents, your abilities, those are all in your DNA put forth by the Lord. He is ours and we are his - family.

Verse 10 (NIV) says the author of our salvation was made "perfect through suffering." Who is the author (some translations may say, captain)?

"Perfect through suffering" at a glance can sound contradictory or like an oxymoron. What does it means?

Why isn't Jesus ashamed to call us family?

Day 2 – Read Hebrews 2: 12-13 NIV

Verses 12-13 are words that were prophesied in Psalm 22:22 and Isaiah 8:17-18. Remember Psalm and Isaiah were written before Christ was born. So they are prophetic words coming true in today's lesson of verses 12-13 in Hebrews 2.

In the previous verses we just learned that it was fitting for Jesus to die on the cross because it's how God was able to reconcile people back to him. God had every right to make that decision as he is the Creator of all things. Because God is holy and he has set us apart we are family. Jesus is not ashamed to call us family. In verse 12-13 it gives examples of what Jesus said regarding us as family, even as brothers. There are four main statements that are applicable to us.

The first is in verse 12 (NIV),

"I will declare your name to my brothers…"

Jesus is saying he will declare God's name to us. We too, as Jesus is our example, are to declare God's name to everyone. We are to share him and show him to our physical family but also to everyone around us. We are not to keep the word stashed away. It was not meant for only certain people to hear, it is for everyone.

The second statement is a continuation of the first and is also in verse 12 (NIV) and says,

"…in the presence of the congregation I will sing your praises."

A congregation could mean a group of people who are all of the same faith gathering but it can also mean a just a general group of people. When he says,

"I will sing your praises…"

We can take it literal and sing about God's goodness. He is certainly worthy of it and that is one expression of worship. But, "to sing someone's praises" is to talk highly of them; to uplift them. So, we are to make known the goodness of God, whether we are literally singing or just having a conversation.

The third statement is in verse 13 (NIV),

"I will put my trust in Him."

Jesus never did anything but the Father's will. Even to death, he knew it was the Father's will and he knew it had to be done for our sake. If there were ever a time he had to trust the Father it was then. We can learn so much from one simple declaration. When we put our trust in something of this earth it's a gamble. It may work out, it may not. We take risk in order to gain reward. When you place your trust in Jesus it is a sure thing. God will work all things together for your good and his glory to those who are called according to his purpose. (Romans 8:28 NIV) This doesn't mean God will give you everything you want. But, even in the hard times, or the times of not understanding his will, he will work it all out. He has a plan a purpose and a direction for your life. He is fighting for you. It is vital that we trust him to see it through.

The last statement in verse 13 (NIV) says,

"Here am I, and the children God has given me."

Jesus is out in the open. He is not hiding. He is not worried about what others think. He is declaring that he is here and he recognizes that his children are from God. He knows we are family. How many times do we say, "Here am I, Lord." How many times do we call out to the Lord wanting to be used by him? Never? Maybe once in a while? After you've hear a particularly moving informational session on hungry children in a third world country? Point being, are we available for God's use and purposes? Are we saying, "Yes, Lord, I'm here, use me."

What's one way Jesus declared God's name to us?

Is there an area of your life you need to trust the Lord more? How can you do this?

Do you tend to be shy when it comes to your faith? Not sure if you should say something to that person? What one are you would like to ask God to use you more? Jot it down and commit it to prayer.

Day 3 – Read Hebrews 2:14-16 NIV

In this section we read why Jesus had to become human. Why couldn't God, being God, just say the word and let the relationship be restored? He could have in his ability, but that wouldn't be an example to us. That wouldn't give us a God who knows what we go through and feels and hurts as we do. Since we are human, flesh and blood, God made Jesus human. If you are to experience something that someone experiences, you need to put yourself in their shoes. You would need to have the same conditions or surroundings. So, Jesus came to this earth as a newborn, to fully experience our life as a human. He did this according to verse 14, to ultimately defeat the devil who holds power over death. But there's also another reason according to this scripture. It was to free us from fear! Everyone has something they are afraid of. Death is a big fear for some. I can only imagine how fearful death must be when you have no idea what the afterlife holds. How frightening it must be to know you will one day die but not know where you go, not know how it's going to feel, does it hurt? Do you go through a tunnel? Do you simply fade off into unconsciousness and cease to exist? God's word says, Jesus came to relieve the fear of death. Because he came and died for us, and defeated death by rising up again on the third day, we get to take part in the result. We don't have to take part in the payment of sin, but we do get the result. And that's first and foremost, everlasting life with the Lord, which is unimaginable to us on earth. Our minds can't even comprehend the beauty and awe of life with him after we leave this earth. But also we are freed from the fear of death. Fear is paralyzing. It can make people stuck and unable to move forward. Jesus became flesh and blood so he could die as a human and take on our penalty of sin to defeat death for us so that we can physically reap the benefit but also mentally reap the benefit of not being fearful.

In verse 14 (NIV) it says, "...he too, _____ in their humanity." What does this word mean and show you about the Lord?

What are the two results of Jesus becoming human and dying as a human according to verses 14-15?

Do you have fear about something in your life? Add it to your prayer list and jot down ways you can overcome it.

Day 4 – Read Hebrews 2:17-18 NIV

Over the last three days we have looked at God sending Jesus to become flesh and blood because you are flesh and blood. God, being the creator and knowing all, knew we would need someone to alleviate our fears and save us from sin in order to restore our relationship to him. Today's lesson is at the heart of this whole week. We've already discussed reasons why Jesus came to earth but these two verses we are going to look at today sums it up and makes God the personable God that he is.

Being that God is a personable God it was necessary for him to come to this earth as a human. There wouldn't be much comfort, to go to God for help in a situation where one feels hurt, betrayed, tempted, whatever it may be, if he was just sitting high and mighty in heaven having never felt the pain of the one hurting. Where's the credibility? Wouldn't one say, "you don't know what it's like…you never lost a child…you were never tempted…you never went without food…you were never betrayed…you were never made fun of…?" On and on our list could go. These are all things that we, as humans, on earth feel. But, it's not that way. God came to this earth in flesh, in human form, to die on the cross of our sins, yes, but that was when he was thirty-three years old. What about the first thirty-three years? He came as a baby so from newborn to thirty-three years old was it easy for him? Did he sail right through life on this earth with no problems? No. He was tempted, he was made fun of, and he was without food. He went through all that so that we can have a God who knows. I am thankful that he knows, not just knows.

There are two kinds of knowledge (actually more, but most things fit into these two). The first is head knowledge. This is when you know something because you read it or it was taught. The second kind is experiential. This knowledge one has because they have experienced it. It goes beyond the head knowledge. It's easy for some people to say, "I understand what you're going through." Depending on the person they are either speaking from head knowledge or experiential knowledge. When someone comprehends what you're going through, they may understand it in terms of conceptualizing it. They know what you're feeling because they see you go through the pain. They hear you talk about it and its painfulness. This is an example of head knowledge and while it can be comforting to have someone there, patting you on the back, giving you a hug, it's not the same as someone with experiential knowledge. When seeking comfort it is much more accepted, relieving and comforting coming from someone with experiential knowledge. You can know for certain that person knows exactly what you're going through. They know your pain, not because you talked about it, but because they have lived it, too. This creates a deeper connection and trust between the two people.

Jesus actually knows from experience, it's not just a head knowledge. Hebrews 2:10 (NIV) says, paraphrased, that it is fitting that he should make our salvation perfect through what he suffered. We discussed this on day one. Why, is it fitting? Because in 2:18 (NIV) it says,

> "Because he himself suffered when he was tempted, he is
> able to help those who are being tempted."

He is qualified. He is able.

He knows how it feels to _____, (you fill in the blank)…to be betrayed…be hurt…lose a loved one…

Describe a situation in which you were able to help someone with head knowledge.

Describe a situation when you were able to help/comfort someone with experiential knowledge.

Which experience was there a tighter connection between the two of you? Why?

If you feel alone in an area or circumstance of your life, say a prayer silently, just between you and Lord. Ask him to help you not feel alone in your circumstance. Whether it be something current or something in the past. If it's in the past ask him to help you get rid of it. Give it to him, that's why he came to earth so he could empathize with you. Ask him to be your comfort knowing you aren't alone and don't have to walk through a dark experience alone. He will get you through.

Day 5 – Reread Hebrews 2:10-18 NIV

This week is chalk full of God's personable characteristics and behavior. How wonderful it is to know we serve a God that is interested and invested in our lives whether it be on this earth or after we die on this earth. This week was all about being in God's family, sending Jesus to help us (in more ways than one), and even as he has ascended back to heaven he knows what we experience and he knows the hurts and pains we feel because of his time on earth. He was our ever present help while he was on earth and he still is even now.

As you reread all of the verses from this week, what's the one thing that stands out to you the most?

What are you most grateful for in these verses?

What will you take away from this week the most?

This Week's Extra Tid-Bit:

Listen to "How Great is our God" by Lincoln Brewster

This Week's Prayers:

_____
_____
_____
_____
_____
_____
_____
_____
_____
_____
_____
_____
_____
_____
_____

This Week's Praises and Thanksgiving:

_____
_____
_____
_____
_____
_____
_____
_____
_____
_____
_____
_____
_____
_____
_____
_____

Lesson 12 (Week 12)

Lean on Him and Walk Straight

If you recall our study last week, we learned about the depths of God's knowing; his understanding. We learned that he came into this world to be able to bear our burdens. Not just physically on the cross, but also as a human living life. Throughout his time on earth he experienced the temptations and anguish we experience. He did it so he could relate to us and be a personal God. This week we're going to talk about trusting God and not ourselves. Keep in mind last week's lesson as we go through this week's. We can trust in him *because* he knows.

Day 1 – Read Proverbs 3:5 NIV

This section of scripture gives an instruction and a result, verse by verse. So, this week we will look at two sections. One verse of instructions, the result and then another verse with instruction and its result.

The first verse to look at has two instructions. The first is to,

"Trust in the Lord with all your heart."

We are to trust in the Lord because like we mentioned last week he is qualified. He is capable. He's the one for the job. It also states we are to do it with every ounce of our being. It says *all* of our heart. This is the part that can be so difficult. Many times we trust in the Lord and want to give over our lives to him, but only in certain areas. We want to maintain control over the areas that benefit us, or that we like because it's convenient, fun or we simply just do not feel he is trustworthy. We want to trust the Lord with our finances even ask the Lord for financial help, but we buy the latest cell phones or get our nails down. I know someone, who a few years ago, was waiting to get her application renewed for welfare, yet she had a freshly painted manicure done. Does this make sense? One would think, that to use the system correctly, this person would be filing papers to renew her welfare because she needed help with finances and the cost of living. And notice I said she was renewing it, it was not a new thing. This was on going, an endless cycle. There was no trying to get off the system and provide for herself. It surely gives off the wrong idea. If someone has a new manicure which would suggest you had extra money, why is she standing in line for help? Is this how we are with the Lord sometimes? Do we pray for financial help, to get out of debt, to have money for the next bill all the while we do not pay our tithes or control our spending of frivolous things? Maybe it's not financial for you. Another example could be entertainment. You are a Christian, but you just love those movies that are inappropriate. As adults, we get to choose what to watch. We get to be mature enough to decide if something should be watched. Do we make the right choices? Are you a Christian but like the "R" rated movies with nothing but violence, foul language and inappropriate clothing, or lack thereof? Like I said, we get a choice. But, let me suggest that if you say you trust in the Lord, take look at your actions and choices in life. Do they reflect you trusting in him? Or are you living contrary? Do you not see fruit in your life even though you pray for a closer relationship to Him? If not, could it be because you aren't fully trusting in him? Are all obstacles and barriers removed so you can trust in him with all your heart?

The second half of verse 5 (NIV) says,

"...and lean not on your own understanding."

So, there are two things we should do. Trust in him and do not trust in ourselves. To lean on your own understanding would be to trust in yourself. That's the opposite of what we are to do. We are to trust in the Lord and *not* lean on our own understanding. Why? Because we don't understand! We know in this world bad things happen. There are diseases, there are abuses of many kinds, there are wars, there is hatred, there is deceit, on and on. There are some things we just don't know "on this side of Heaven" as they say. We know the overall plan of God but sometimes we can't see the intricacies of it as it unfolds on earth. He gives us pieces. He gives us his word. But, in your life, day to day, there are things happening that sometimes don't make sense. We can trust that the Lord knows what he is doing. He will use it for his glory even when we don't understand.

What are the two verbs in this verse that describe our role? (One is a singular verb and one is a verb phrase)

This lesson touched on it, but describe further in your opinion, why we cannot lean on our own understanding?

Is there an area you feel you currently have trouble trusting the Lord?

Has there been a situation in your life that you did tried to understand through your own knowledge or understanding? How does leaning on God compare to leaning on ourselves?

Day 2 - Read Proverbs 3:6 NIV

Trusting in the Lord and not ourselves can be difficult when we don't seek the Lord. When we don't stay close to the Lord it's easy to begin to think we have things under control and we lean on our own understanding. Today we will discuss one more instruction and then see the result that occurs if we do these things.

This first part of verse 6 (NIV) says,

"...in all your ways acknowledge him."

So, in the previous verse we saw that we are to trust in the Lord with *all* of our heart and in verse 6 we see we are to acknowledge him in *all* our ways. The Lord wants us to be committed in *all* areas. This is not a "needy" thing on his part. This is not a "selfish" reason on the Lord's part. It is so he can work through you. If he doesn't have your whole heart, then the world does. If he doesn't have every part of your life: your marriage, your finances, your attitude, your kids, your work, and then the world has some part of it. My former pastor, whom I am so grateful for, always made the church question critically whether or not partial obedience is obedience. Can we acknowledge the Lord only in some areas of our life but not in others and still be living in obedience to him? Can we say I gave ten percent at church on Sunday, get drunk but think we are living in obedience? "Well I gave ten percent...so it doesn't matter how I spent the rest of my money." Does one obedient act excuse the other non-obedient act? Is partial obedience even obedience at all?

The second part of the verse gives us the result. So far in this week's lessons we've seen three instructions. The result for those instructions is,

"...and he will make your paths straight."

Yesterday's lesson and today's lesson are one continuous thought. When you look at your text there aren't any periods, ending the thought, in verse 5 or 6 until you get to the end of 6. So, each of these three instructions and result go together. For the sake of discussion we have broken it down into two parts (yesterday and today).

If we trust in him, do not look to our own understanding and acknowledge him in everything then...

"He will make our paths straight."

This is not only a result for what will happen, but is a definitive statement. The word, "will," is definitive. It is for sure. You can count on it. It's not a word that is indecisive. He will do it. Another thing to notice about the word, "will," is it is futuristic. He will do it, but only after the previous remarks are met. So, he will make our paths straight, only once we trust in him, lean on him and acknowledge him. God is not asking us to be perfect before he comes to us. Be sure you are clear on this. He is not saying to be without issues or faults when we live for him. The three requirements of trust him, lean on him and acknowledge him are all that of attitude and mindset. They are not physical things you have to do. Sure, there may be outwardly, physical gestures or actions that happen because of these elements, but the elements themselves are a decision we make in our head, our mind and our heart. If you have the right motive in your heart, the right mindset and willingness to be used by God, then he will use you. He does not call those that are perfect, just willing. He will then transform you into something new. What does "make our paths straight" mean? He will guide us and keep us on the right road. When we are close to the Lord it is much more difficult to stray from him. When we slack in our relationship with him, stop reading the Bible, stop going to church, start watching that TV show again that you stopped because you know it wasn't edifying the Lord or taking a drink when you hadn't in months or years, these all lead to wondering off. The metaphor is a road. When we walk with the Lord we stay on the right road. When we put distance between him and us we begin to take wrong turns or we get lost. But, the Lord says he will make our paths straight, he will keep us on the road. So, how/when will he do this? When we trust him, lean on him and acknowledge him. Our paths do not become straight by God following us. We trust and follow him and then our paths are straight.

Taking into account day one and day two what are the three things we need to do?

1.
2.
3.

What does God do, if we do those three things?

Often, people want to say, if the Lord shows me, I will trust him or believe him? Is this correct? According to the verses we studied the last two days, our decision needs to happen before God's action. We need to trust him, lean on him not ourselves and acknowledge him before he will direct. Why is this?

Once we've trusted him, leaned on him (not ourselves) and acknowledged him once is that it? Or does it need to happen often: monthly, weekly, daily?

Day 3 – Read Proverbs 3:7 NIV

Day one and two talked about the first set of instructions and its result. Today (instructions) and tomorrow (result) we will talk about the second. This set of instructions also has three just as in day one and two.

Just like in verse 5 (NIV) the Lord says,

"...lean not on your own understanding..."

In verse 7 he says,

"Do not be wise in your own eyes..."

More than once now, the Lord warns us against ourselves. Anything the Lord says is important, but if he repeats it, he knows we need to hear it again. He knows it is a potential issue for us, so he reminds us or states it in a different way. Two days ago, in our lesson, he told us not to put much stake into our own understanding, now he tells us not to think we are all that wise. Sometimes it is easy to get caught up in thinking we have the Lord figured out. We become arrogant, conceded. This is a dangerous place to be because we begin to take credit. We think we have created the life we have. We think our money is ours, we think we got ourselves through difficult times. We become more dependent on ourselves and less dependent on God. Sometimes, we even think we need to help the Lord. We don't. We need to realize that we do not have it all together, but the Lord does. He holds every little bit of this world together. He continuously draws us closer to him and we (hopefully and part of the point of this study guide) are always growing in our knowledge and love for him, but we will never comprehend the full extent of God while on this earth. We cannot become so foolish as to think we are smart enough to run our own lives. As human, just because of our nature of being human, because of being descendants from Adam and Eve, we will make mistakes. We will and do sin. We make wrongs choices, bad decisions. The Lord doesn't. He doesn't do any of that. He is a perfect God who wants to help his children.

The second part of the verse is our second and third instruction and it says,

"...fear the Lord and shun evil."

The word fear is not a frightful, scared or hide-under-the-covers fear. It is a reverence. It is a respectful fear. Out of reverence, out of his authority we fear the Lord. We are to have this kind of fear. We are to respect God. We are to understand he is in authority. The next part of that same phrase says to put off evil. "Shun" it. The word "shun" means to persistently avoid, ignore or reject. We are to <u>avoid</u> it. We are not to go seek it out or purposely put ourselves in a situation of evil. We are also to <u>ignore</u> it. When the devil wants to try to bring up something you know the Lord has forgiven or a habit in your life that you have conquered, do not play into it. Do not let the devil begin to tempt you into thinking the sin or the behavior is not atoned for. Also the definition says <u>reject</u>. Not only are we to ignore it but we are to reject it. Rejecting something requires an action. We have to purposely say no to it. When you ignore something you don't have to respond at all. But, when you reject something there is an action involved. Even if it's an action involving your mindset. You push it away. You dismiss it as having no worth or value. That is how we are to deal with evil. The definition of "shun" began with an adverb. This describes the verb (s) which are avoid, ignore, reject. It says to do this persistently. When dealing with the devil he is persistent. He will keep coming back to wear you down. This is why it is so important to walk with the Lord daily. To be reading his word daily. So our response then is not only to avoid evil, ignore evil and reject evil but to do it persistently. Because evil is persistent. We need to combat it persistently. Tomorrow we will see what this combination of fearing the Lord and shunning evil along with not being wise to ourselves can lead to.

Think of or research someone in the Bible who became arrogant and wise in their own eyes. How/why did they do this and what was the result?

Why does the Lord keep warning us about ourselves?

Why do we sometimes fall into thinking we need to "help" God?

Day 4 – Read Proverbs 3:8 NIV

Today we will look at the result of yesterday's instructions. Yesterday's instructions were from Proverbs 3:7 (NIV) and said to,

"Not be wise in our own eyes…"

And

"Fear the Lord and shun evil."

When we do these three things verse 8 tells us it,

"…will bring health to your body and nourishment to you bones."

This sounds like physical health. We know that the Lord is in control of our physical health, though we do have a responsibility to treat our bodies in a healthy manner. We also know that the Lord is the ultimate healer when something is wrong in our bodies. When we look at this verse from a physical standpoint, we will see that when you stop thinking that you are in control, stop being so wise in your own eyes, which really makes you foolish, and you allow God to be in charge of your life the stress naturally melts away. We are still people who still live in this world. So, there will still be stress, there will still be difficult times, but when we give those times and our day to day life when things seem fine, over to the Lord it lifts a burden off our shoulders that the Lord intends to carry, not us. As a result there is a healthier you. So, yes, there can be a physical application in this verse.

There is also a spiritual application. We know that Lord washes us clean. He takes the dirtiness and wipes it away. He is the living water. The word says when you drink of this water you will never thirst again (John 4:10-14 NIV). So when you fear the Lord and shun evil, as well as seek the Lord's wisdom, not your own, he will give you what you need to be sustained. He will sustain your body and mind. Not only this, but Proverbs 4:22 (NIV) says that the Lord's words are,

"Life…health to his whole body."

Jesus's words are the very life that we need. His words, his wisdom, his guidance and directions, are the very life giving substance that we need to be healthy spiritually.

In what way do you need to be healthier today, physically or spiritually?

How can you seek out this healthier body and spirit?

What are the three ways you can "bring health to your body and nourishment to you bones?"(Think back to yesterday's lesson)

Day 5 – Recap each day this week Read Proverbs 3:5-8 NIV

"Trust in the _____ with _____ your heart and lean _____ on your own understanding; in _____ your ways acknowledge _____, and he will make your paths _____. Do not be _____ in your own eyes; _____ the _____ and shun evil. This will bring _____ to your body and _____ to your bones."

What's one way you will acknowledge the Lord over the next couple of days that maybe you haven't done so in the past?

How can you lean of God instead of yourself from now on?

Why is it important to fear the Lord?

Who, in the Bible do you admire to because of their fear of the Lord? Why?

This Week's Extra Tid-Bit:

Listen to "Sovereign" by Chris Tomlin

This Week's Prayers:

_____
_____
_____
_____
_____
_____
_____
_____
_____
_____
_____
_____
_____
_____
_____
_____
_____

This Week's Praises and Thanksgiving:

_____
_____
_____
_____
_____
_____
_____
_____
_____
_____
_____
_____
_____
_____
_____
_____
_____
_____

Lesson 13 (week 13)

Divided

As is with previous lessons, this week is an extension and builds upon last week. Last week we learned that we need to trust the Lord and not ourselves. We need to be cautious of our own pride and thinking that we have it all figured out, or worse, thinking we need to "help" God. This week we will look at some of the ways the enemy tries to creep in to cause destruction. We'll look at reasons why, in addition to last week's reasons, we need to lean on him and trust him. We will see that the enemy seeks to divide us and what the Lord says about it.

Day 1 – Read Matthew 12:25 NIV

Jesus just healed a man who was demon-possessed, blind and mute. The people were questioning if this truly was the Son of David, but the Pharisees were accusing him of being Beelzebub, the Prince of Demons or Satan, himself. This starts a whole slew teaching and application from Jesus. We will start with verse 25 today, but even to the end of this section you will see how this scenario is very key in what not to do. Once they made these claims, Jesus responded with the following:

"Jesus knew their thoughts and said to them, 'Every kingdom divided against itself will be ruined, and every city or household divided against itself will not stand.'"

We are God's creation. God's children. God's beloved. Satan wants to destroy anything that is good and of God. Therefore, Satan wants to destroy us, each person. "Us" does not refer to one people group, such as just unbelievers or believers, I'm talking about all people, all mankind. He does this in different ways. It can be obvious such as the molesters, murders, thieves, etc. These people obviously have made a wrong turn in life and allowed the enemy to influence them. But he also destroys people in subtle ways, too. The friend from work who gives you a ride to work every day that slowly becomes more than a friend then an affair happens, missing a couple weeks at church then before you know it, it's been a couple months, now you don't go anymore. It could be keeping you so busy with things that seem right and good that you don't notice or put any effort into the things of God anymore. These are all ways the enemy wants to and is destroying people. But, there's another way that is important for us to recognize and understand. With understanding the change can come that we so desperately need.

Satan attacks from within. On a big scale, from within nations, on a smaller scale, within cities and even a smaller more intimate setting, the household and family. He gets in and causes chaos and destruction from within. Let's look at each of these briefly.

Our nation used to stand united as one under God, as the pledge to our flag says. Is this still true or are we a nation torn? In shambles. Divided. We struggle so hard to make things better, more profitable, more equal. In reality, are we destroying ourselves from the inside out?

On a slightly smaller scale, he attacks our cities and communities. More and more crime, joblessness within our towns and cities. Ma and Pa shops closing everywhere, not enough emergency responders. Teachers without proper supplies and aren't given the freedom to actually teach. You can't hardly trust your own neighbor anymore. It seems there are more quarrels over non-essential things with neighbors than ever before. What happen to love you neighbor, treat people the way you want to be treated and all the good ol' lessons of life?

Then he (Satan) really goes for the blow. He is attacking our families and our households. This is attacking from within at its core. Husbands and wives are fighting on a regular basis, many times not even in a relationship anymore, but holding it together until the kids are eighteen. The kids are being raised by two different people who aren't on the same page for parenting. So, they get different teachings, discipline (if that even exists), and different expectations. And this is all assuming there's two parents at home. Often there is not. Satan knows this…he's part of the cause. So, now there's single parents everywhere most doing their best. But, it's not a one man job. Kids can grow up healthy and making good choices with single parents, that's not at all what I'm saying. There are lots of single parents who are doing a wonderful job. I'm saying there's still a void in that situation, for the children and the parent. So, even though they may be a healthy, happy family, Satan is happy with the disruption in their lives. He only needs a subtle disruption. He is happy to have caused some sort of chaos even if they seem to be adjusting well.

So, what is it we are to do? We need to recognize the tricks of Satan. We need to call him out on it and seek God to fight our battles. Going through a difficult time a few years ago, I was praying with my Pastor. In the prayer he said I needed to let God fight for me. Let him be my champion. That really stuck with me. God fights for us. He intercedes to the Father for us. He breaks chains, takes blinders off and gives us freedom. If you find yourself in a situation of being divided or at odds with someone take it God. Let him be your champion. He will.

What's one way in the past or currently you can see Satan at work, trying to divide you with someone else whether it be your spouse, employer, family member or another?

What was the outcome of Satan's attempt? Did he succeed or did you recognize it and ask God for help? If something is still going on right now, how can you not be divided?

In this verse, Jesus says that every kingdom divided against…? Against another kingdom?

Since Jesus says, "every kingdom divided against <u>itself</u> will be ruined…" could this explain the divorce rate, at least in part?

Day 2 – Read Matthew 12:26-29 NIV

Through these four verses, Jesus gives examples of how a kingdom or nation will fall by being divided against itself. He starts with the example of,

"…if Satan drives out Satan…"

The result if Satan drives out Satan would be division against himself. He would be destroying himself. Jesus raises the question,

"How can his kingdom stand?"

If Satan drives himself out what/who is left to further his kingdom and ensure it stands? Nothing. He is the source, the leader of his kingdom, therefore if he goes, all else that would potentially follow him would not stand as well, but fall.

Jesus also gives the example of him driving out demons by the Spirit of God. This is not a kingdom divided against itself. This is opposite; one driving out the other. When there are two opponents, one falls and one is victorious. Since they were in opposition there is not kingdom that gets divided, only one that falls. So, Jesus says in verse 28,

"But if I drive out demons by the Spirit of God, then the kingdom of God has come upon you."

His final example in this passage is that of a strong man's house being robbed. He asks, how would a strong man's house be robbed if the strong man is home? If he is home, his house is protected. He is watching his possessions and guarding them. Only when the strong man is tied up can he be robbed. When tied up, he is bound. He can't move or stop the thieves. At which point it is as if his house is divided against him. They are no longer "working together." Something has come in and disrupted the "flow" of the household.

Sometimes, Satan disrupts households in a very subtle manner and sometimes in an obvious manner. Can you think of someone in the Bible that became divided against him/herself, his/ her family or his kingdom? Write the scripture reference and a brief description.

How did the situation turn out for who you listed in the previous question?

What can you learn from that person's experience?

Day 3 – Read Matthew 12:30-32 NIV

So far this week, in this passage of scripture in Matthew 12, we have seen Jesus speak plainly that one divided against itself cannot stand. This could be a large scale such as a nation or a small scale such as a family or household. Jesus gives us examples and then in verses 30-32, he warns us of a very serious sin that happened back in verse 24.

Jesus prefaces, the warning of the sin by stating,

"He who is not with me is against me…"

Our world would like to think there are many ways to heaven. Our culture would like to think that there is more than one god; it's just whatever each individual wants to believe. But, John 14:6 (NIV) and Matthew 7:14 (NIV) tell us it's not so. Jesus is the only one. The only true God and only way to heaven. Because of this, we know that what he says in verse 30 is true.

"He who is not with me is against me…"

There are only two options in life regarding your beliefs. You are either for God or not. There are two camps, those in God's camp and everyone else. Christians take the heat for this, being called names like narrow minded, but God's word is clear.

So, he then goes on to state the sin in which we are warned. All sins in the entire world can be forgiven. Even the worst sin imaginable can be forgiven when a repentant heart asks. But, the sin of blasphemy against the Holy Spirit cannot be forgiven. Jesus, in verse 24, has just heard the people claim that the only way Jesus healed the man was through a Beelzebub, which is Satan. The people were speaking evil of the Holy Spirit, claiming Jesus had evil power in him. This is the only sin that cannot be forgiven. Jesus knew the people's heart, intensions and motives. He also knew what he heard and who he was and still is. To mock, make fun of and state such a serious claim against the Holy Spirit is not something the Lord forgives. These people do not have the authority to make such claims. The verses we will look at tomorrow will give us more insight as to how and why Jesus takes what these people said very seriously and why we are to watch what we say.

Who were the people in verses 23-24 that made the claim?

Why did he follow their claim with verse 25? He heard their thoughts and then went right into talking about a kingdom divided against itself. Are they connected?

We talked about the first part of verse 30 (NIV), "He who is not with me is against me..." What does the second half of that verse say and what does it mean?

Day 4 – Read Matthew 12:33-36 NIV

In this section we see how the Lord knows that these people who blasphemed the Holy Spirit had bad intensions and why he addresses it so seriously. Of course, he's God, so he is omniscient not to mention he literally heard their comments. However, there is also a practical way he knew and one we can learn from as well.

He compares people with that of trees. A healthy tree, a good tree, one that is planted firmly in the ground will produce fruit. And it will produce the right kind of fruit and it will be good fruit. He says, in verse thirty-three, that a tree is recognized by its fruit. So, if there is a bad tree it will produce bad fruit. And the opposite is true as well. The Lord could recognize these people's heart and true intensions because of their actions, because of the words they spoke. If the people were "good trees" they would "produce good fruit." But, that's not what happened. He goes on to say in verse 34 (NIV),

> "…how can you who are evil say anything good?"

He knew they were evil. He knew their intensions. And it was proven by their actions. Also, in verse 34 is a very important lesson we can learn. Jesus says,

> "…for out of the overflow of the heart the mouth speaks."

It is so important that we watch what we say. Have you ever been so mad that you said something that was too harsh? Or maybe something you'd been wanting to say, but never had the courage to do so until you were really upset. It's because when our emotions get stirred up our true thoughts and intensions rise up. What we're really feeling comes out in these situations. It's not always a negative effect, though. Our heart may be filled with a tremendous amount of gratitude and thankfulness. Because of this, we speak words of thanks and appreciation. Whatever is truly in our heart will come out. In this case, however, this is both a warning as well as a truth that we need to understand about ourselves and other people.

In verse 36, Jesus warns us that everyone will one day, give an account for every word they have spoken. What adjective is used in your Bible to describe the word, "word?" Write it here:

In my version (NIV) it says "careless." Everyone,

> "…will give account on the day of judgment for every careless word they have spoken."

150

It is so easy sometimes to not pay attention to the words we speak. But, the Lord takes it seriously. We are to watch what we say. Are we lifting others up with our speech? Are we standing up for what is right with our speech? Or, are we putting others down? Are we using words that do not edify the Lord? The Lord calls this type of speech, "careless." Lack of caring. Do we care about what we say? This is something we need to think about and consider.

Today, pay extra attention to what you say and how you say it. Give particular notice to anything you say that may not be of God or edifying to him and ask him in prayer to help you improve in this area.

Has anyone ever said something to you that put you down or hurt your feelings? How did it make you feel?

Is that how God intends for us to talk to each other? Why not?

Have you been the one to say inappropriate things or hurtful things? How did it make you feel?

What's one way that you can ask the Lord to help you speak appropriately? Give more compliments? Less complaining? Quit saying curse words? Add it to your prayer list and commit it to prayer.

Day 5 – Read Matthew 12:37 NIV

This is the last verse for this week and in this section. I left it to its own study on day five because it sums up Jesus's lesson and offers us a warning and a choice. Matthew 12:37 (NIV) says,

"For by your words you will be acquitted, and by your words you will be condemned."

We are given two choices. We can be acquitted or we can be condemned. We are either acquitted by what we say or we can be condemned by what we say. This has a twofold application. The first is that of your everyday talk. What you say, what is the overflow of your heart that comes out of your mouth each day. When you talk appropriately you lift Jesus up. When you don't talk appropriately you are spreading bad seed. You are of a "bad tree" producing "bad fruit."

The second application is how we are saved and have eternal life. We are saved by believing in the finished work of the cross and resurrection. It is by our <u>words</u> that we confess this belief. So, you are literally acquitted of all counts of sin when you choose to confess your need for Jesus as your Lord and Savior. If one should choose not to believe in the Lord for salvation, he is condemned and his sin is still upon him resulting in eternal death.

Our words are very important. Words can go either way, acquit or condemn. It's our choice.

What does Romans 10:9 say?

How is it that we are saved? Believe in our heart and …..?

On day one this week we talked about a kingdom, nation or house divided against itself. We looked at examples and saw that it can't stand. That verse was really the cornerstone of this whole week. The rest of the week was built from that verse according to how Jesus gave the lesson. How does the lesson about our words tie into day one?

<u>*This Week's Extra Tid-Bits:*</u>

"But if serving the Lord seems undesirable to you, then choose for yourselves this day whom you will serve...But as for me and my household we will serve the Lord." Joshua 24:15

Listen to "Slow Fade" by Casting Crowns

This Week's Prayers:

_____
_____
_____
_____
_____
_____
_____
_____
_____
_____
_____
_____
_____
_____
_____

This Week's Praises and Thanksgiving:

_____
_____
_____
_____
_____
_____
_____
_____
_____
_____
_____
_____
_____
_____

Lesson 14 (Week 14)

Forever Love

Last week was filled with some important truths and warnings. We saw that a kingdom can't stand when it is divided against itself. We saw that blasphemy of the Holy Spirit is an unforgivable sin. And finally, we saw that the words we speak are very important and hold a lot of weight. I hope it encouraged you to recognize when the enemy is at work and to turn to Jesus no matter what the circumstance in your life. He is the one we trust. He is the one that will direct our paths and it's not just for a time. He will always faithful, he will always be our champion. He will always love us and be for us. I hope you find more encouragement in this week's lesson about God's unending love for us; the simple yet powerful truth that nothing can separate us from his love!

Day 1 – Read Romans 8:31-32 NIV

Paul asks a very important question in verse 31. What is this question?

In these verses, Paul is making the point that God has done all these things for us. He gave up his son. This is the ultimate sacrifice anyone could possibly make. So, if he did this for us, don't we realize how much he cares for us and will give us all things along with Jesus (Romans 8:32)? The Bible says, just a few verses back in Romans 8:17 (NIV) that we are co heirs with Christ because we are the children of God. In 1 Peter 2:9 (NIV) it says we are a royal priest hood and because of this we are to declare his praises for what he's done.

So, what's the answer to Paul's question?

It is humbling to realize, to really grasp that we have God on our side. To really let it sink in that God fights our battles, the king of all kings. There is no other name higher than that of Christ. Philippians 2:9 (NIV) says that God gave him a name that is above all names. This is the one who, on a daily basis, fights for you. He wards off spiritual demons we don't even know about. And in our temptations and weaknesses that we do know about, he fights for us there, too. He gives us strength to overcome, he gives us grace to start a new day.

If God is for us, who can be against us?

What word used to describe how God gives us all things in verse 32?

He is happy to make us co heirs with Christ. He *graciously* gives it. The word "graciously" does not mean rude or impolite. On the contrary, it means, hospitable, polite, caring. God gives us to be co heirs with Christ in a caring way. In a polite and affectionate way. It is on purpose. He willed it to be. Because of all this, we can see that God loves us and is for us. God, being the highest of the high, being in all authority over any earthy authority is for us.

If God is for us, who can be against us?

"Give us all things" does not mean we can ask for anything and we will get it. It doesn't mean you can expect God to make you rich, if we have money trouble. It doesn't mean you'll wake up one morning with a brand new car in your driveway because you wanted one. It doesn't even mean you will automatically get the job you applied for because you asked God. God still governs our life in a sovereign way. When we are in him, not everything is in his will. I'm sure most people would like a brand new car, but if it's not in his will then it won't happen. I'm sure most people would like more money, even if they don't want to be rich. But, that's not always in his will. It doesn't mean he won't make a way to provide, but it's all within what he sees fit. When we are in Christ, we give him control over our lives. He will take care of us, he will provide for us. So, what does "give us all things" mean then? This is an inheritance. We will inherit life in heaven, where we will be with Christ forever and reap rewards (Ephesians 1:11 NIV, 1 Peter 1:4 NIV). So, we can have benefits and blessings on earth but the real implication of being co heirs with Christ is in heaven. After all, the Bible says he is preparing a place for you (John 14:2-3 NIV). It is for you. You partake in this place, it is your inheritance.

What does knowing God is for you, do to your attitude?

What are situations you might be in this week that remembering God is for you will help? Do you have a tough meeting coming up? An interview? A doctor's appointment? Conference with your child's teacher?

We always say that the devil is against us. He's out to destroy us. How is this if God is for us? In other words, if the answer to "who can be against us", is no one, then how can the enemy be against us? Explain and clarify.

Day 2 – Read Romans 8: 33-34 NIV

It is well established in yesterday's verses that God is very much for us. He gave his only Son for us which is the greatest expression of love. That being true, how much more willing is he to have us be co heirs with Christ? These verses are powerful in that they show us who we are in Christ and his love for us. Today, we continue the same thought.

If God is the ultimate authority, the Word says in Romans 8:33-34 (NIV),

"Who will bring any charge against those whom God has chosen?"

"Who is he that condemns?"

Can anyone charge you and me other than God? On earth, we have governments, judges and a legal system. We are to abide by the law, we are to pay taxes and we are to be respectful citizens of our world. So, though we may break a law on earth and be charged by a judge, or a police officer with breaking that law, it is only temporary. It is only for a time that, that judgment is against us. It is not the final authority. This kind of judgment is only an earthly judgment. God, judges the heart and our actions and our responses to the knowledge we have here on earth. He is the One who can save us. And since he has saved us, we are longer guilty. You or I may have been guilty about that speeding ticket, or may have ran a stop sign we didn't see, so we paid the fine and took traffic school. We paid the penalty. With God, concerning our eternity, He paid our penalty. We are no longer guilty. So, who can charge us or condemn us? God is the only rightful judge. And when you are in him, you are not condemned.

The last part of verse 34 (NIV) says,

"…and is also interceding for us."

So far, we have established that God loves us so much he gives us an inheritance, he does not let anyone have the authority in condemning you and now we see that he is also interceding for us. Not only is he our help on earth, but he goes to the Father, in heaven, on our behalf and pleads our case. He goes to the Father and fights for us. 1 John 2:1 (NIV) says he is our advocate. An advocate is someone who is stepping in the gap for another, someone who is defending another. This is what Jesus does for you and me. He steps in for us and defends us.

"If God is for us, who can be against us?"

What are the three things this week's lesson has established so far in knowing that nothing can separate us from the love of God.

1.
2.
3.

Who is an advocate/what does an advocate do?

Who is our advocate?

What are some things you need Jesus to advocate for you about? Commit them to your prayer list and pray about these things.

Day 3 – Read Romans 8: 35-36 NIV

God has established his loyalty, if you will, to us in the last few days of study through Romans 8:31-34 (NIV). Today we continue with examples of just how powerful and strong is his love. Verse 35 starts out with another question. This question is the culminating question for this whole week. Take note of it and write it here:

The love of Christ is so strong that nothing can separate us from it. God will always love you and always has. Romans 5:8 (NIV) tells us that Christ died for us even while we were still sinners. And to die for us is to show love at its deepest. There is a list of circumstances Paul lists when asking if anything can separate us from the love of Christ. Let's look at each circumstance, think about yourself in these circumstances and Christ's love for you.

The first circumstance is trouble. Can trouble separate us from the love of Christ? Can you get yourself into so much trouble with the law, your parents, your spouse, your employer than God can't and won't love you anymore? What's your thoughts? Jot them down here:

The second circumstance is hardship. Maybe you have a financial hardship. Maybe it's bankruptcy. Does this make God love you any less? Maybe you're going through a hardship with your parents or in laws. Does God stop loving you? What's your thoughts? Jot them down here:

The next circumstance is persecution. Have you been persecuted for your beliefs? Did God say it would be easy being a Christian? He didn't say it would be easy, but he did promise to be with you. Have you ever been persecuted for doing the right thing when everyone else around you was putting pressure on you to do the wrong thing? Does this change how God loves you? Does it separate you from his love? Or does it possibly draw you closer to him? What are your thoughts? Jot them down here:

The next circumstance is famine or nakedness. Does God love you based on your money? Based on how much "stuff" you have? If you are rich, he loves you. If you are poor he loves you. Life has valleys. In the times of plenty does he love you more than the times you were in need? How does He direct us to use our money and whether or not we obey that, does it affect his love for us? What are your thoughts? Jot them down here:

The last circumstance Paul mentions is danger or the sword. There will come a time where you may be faced with danger. How is or will God's love be demonstrated to you in these times? Can dangerous times separate you from the love of Christ? Can we make bad choices during such times that will separate us? What are your thoughts? Jot them down here:

Finally, verse 36 refers to trouble in the world. There will always be trouble in the world. The world itself, the creation of the earth is a beautiful place designed to give us everything we need to be sustained. However, because of sin, what's in the world is corrupt. It's full of hatred, murderers, liars, cheaters and so on. Because of this we know we too, will go through hard times, but we stand for the love of Christ. This verse is almost a dreary one. It leaves us feeling like we are defeated. But, we know that's not the case. Tomorrow we will see Paul's response.

Day 4 – Read Romans 8:37-39 NIV

Up to this point, all Paul's questions have been rhetorical, they are questions meant to get you and me thinking. Once he's pleaded his case of Christ's love, he answers the questions himself. In verse 37, he responds to verse 36 which said that we,

> "…face death all day long."

It's almost a defeated attitude. It's the woes of this world. But, Paul quickly corrects the attitude and says,

> "No."

It is important that we distinguish what Paul is correcting here. He is not correcting God's word. He wrote this section of scripture through the Holy Spirit's guidance, so exactly what the Lord wanted to be written is written. Paul is correctly the thought process that the people might be having from that verse. Verse 36, though it sounds dreary of one of defeat is actually to show how we've overcome that situation. After his exclamation of no, Paul continues on. He says,

> "…in all these things we are more than conquerors through him who loved us."

We are not just conquerors, we are <u>more</u> than conquerors through Christ. He then tells us of all the things that cannot separate us from the love of God through Christ. Jot down each things he says:

You'll notice at the end of his list he says,

> "…nor anything else in all creation…"

There is not one single circumstance, situation, family member, employer, government, law or anything else than separate us from the love of God. It's amazing to think about. And it gives us great comfort. No matter what is going on in your world, or the world in which we all live, nothing will ever separate us from his love!

The beginning of verse 38, Paul says,

"For I am convinced..."

Who does the convincing? Do we convince ourselves that God is real, that he is love, and that we need him to save us? By the way, the word, "convince" is not one of deception, it's one of making an informed choice after weighing the information.

Why might God have chosen Paul to write this book of Romans and specially these verses we've looked at this week?

Day 5 – Read Romans 8:31-39 NIV

For the last four days we have been going through various situations found in verses 31-36. We have looked at the situations and thought about how each one impacts Christ's love for us. Paul used a lot of questions in these verses to appeal to the reader. He wants you and me to think about these things. He wants us to be convinced of them because they are truths. In verses 37-39, Paul answers his own questions he set forth throughout the previous verses.

Right away, in verse 37 (NIV) he says,

"No…"

You'll remember from the previous verses he has been asking a mired of different questions to get you thinking if there is anything that can separate you from the love of Christ. He finally answers it with, no! There's not. Christ's love is so strong that nothing can separate us from it. In verses 38-39 he sums up all the little situations discussed before with overall categories of what cannot separate us from his love. Anything, anyone can ever think of can fit into one of these categories.

All of life's situations can be summed up in which categories (found in verses 38-39):

Paul says how many of these can separate us from the love of God?

Having confidence of this ourselves, how should we live our lives?

<u>*This Week's Extra Tid-Bits:*</u>

Suggested songs to listen to:

"Whom Shall I Fear" by Chris Tomlin

"Nothing Ever (Could Separate Us)" by Citizen Way

"How Can it Be" by Lauren Daigle

This Week's Prayers:

_____
_____
_____
_____
_____
_____
_____
_____
_____
_____
_____
_____
_____
_____
_____
_____

This Week's Praises and Thanksgiving:

_____
_____
_____
_____
_____
_____
_____
_____
_____
_____
_____
_____
_____
_____
_____
_____
_____
_____
_____

Lesson 15 (Week 15)

Bread of Life

The message of the Gospel is so incredibly simple. In Luke 18, Matthew 19 and Mark 10, children were coming to Jesus and the disciples were telling the children to leave him alone, but Jesus cares for children just as adults. He wanted them to come. They sat with him and he taught the children and they could understand. This is the simplicity of the Good News. The Bible is filled with analogies, stories, people's lives, parables, sin, betrayal, and even crucifixion. So, the Bible is not always easy to read, but the Gospel is very simple to understand. The Gospel is simply the Good News. This week, we will explore Jesus as the Bread of Life. He is complex; fully human and fully God, yet so simple a child can understand and come to him. He sustains us and gives us life.

Day 1 – Read John 6:25-27 NIV

In verse 27 Jesus is speaking and he says,

> "Do not work for food that spoils, but for food that endures
> eternal life, which the Son of Man will give you."

This verse tells us what we should be doing in life. So many people get caught up in having things. Having stuff. They work hard every day just to have more of this and more of that. Work is good. We are to work and earn our wages for living. There's nothing wrong in wanting things so long as our focus is not skewed. Jesus said,

> "Do not work for food that spoils…"

The things of this earth that we work for will spoil. Not just literal food left in the refrigerator too long, but your material possessions. He says to work for food that endures eternal life. So instead of spending all our energy, time and resources on material, temporary things, we are to spend it on eternal things. What does this look like? Invest in people's lives. Take time to share the Good News with people. Let Christ shine through you, through your attitude and actions. Be sure that the things of God are more important to you than things of this world. How you live your life will be proof of this.

Which areas in your life do you need to focus more on the eternal things of God? Put them in this week's prayers.

What are some ways you can accomplish this?

The end of verse 27 says that God the Father has placed his seal of approval on Jesus. Placing a seal on something shows that it is taken. It shows ownership. The Romans used to seal their letters or scrolls with a seal that consisted of wax and would say the person's name, showing ownership. A seal can also show that something is done, permanent, it's claimed. When you seal a letter to send in the mail, the letter does not get out until the person receiving it opens it. The contents are kept safe inside because it is sealed. God the Father, has approved Jesus the Son, with his seal. He has given Jesus authority.

Our response to Jesus should be that of wanting God to put his seal on us. There's a hymn called, "Come Thou Fount of Every Blessing." I encourage you to look up the lyrics. They are brilliant lyrics. One of the key words is "prone," as shown from this synopsis:

"Prone to wonder, Lord I feel it,
prone to leave the God I love
here's my heart Lord, take and seal it,
seal it for thy courts above"

What does "prone" mean?

Given the definition you found, what does this statement mean? Does that mean we don't know God? Does that mean we aren't really a believer? No. It means we have faulty hearts, and we can get caught up in the things of this world. God warns us not to do that. He warns us that the things of this world will spoil. These lyrics are a plea to God. For me, I think like many others, it's a recognition of knowing I am a sinner, of knowing I tend to wonder. So, my plea to God is to take my heart and keep only for God. It's a cry. If God seals my heart to him and for his purposes, then it is done. I am his. It's my prayer. I hope that it is yours, too.

Do some research on the word, "seal." Find examples and information about general definitions of something being sealed but also Biblical meanings. Search scriptures and see if you can come up with other verses discussing a seal. Write it here and discuss when it's used, how it's used and its meaning.

Compare your answers to the above question with those in your group and discuss what it is to be sealed.

Day 2 – Read John 6:28-34 NIV

The disciples go on to ask in verse 28,

> "What must we do to do the works of God?"

And Jesus's answer in verse 29 sums it up.

> "The work of God is this: to believe in the one he has sent."

Here's the simplicity I mentioned in the introduction of this lesson. Salvation - eternal life, does not come from works. You cannot work your way to heaven. You cannot even earn your way to eternal life in heaven. Apart from the Lord you cannot be good enough. Jesus's words were to <u>believe</u> in him. That's it. Ephesians 2:8 (NIV) says,

> "For it is by grace you have been saved, through faith – and
> this is not from yourselves, it is the gift of God."

You are saved by grace because you have faith. There is a response to one's belief. Because one believes in the Lord you will see works being done. You will see the person's life changed. But, it is not because of these things that they are saved, it's merely a result. One is saved by God's grace through faith. Rest in the fact that we don't have to try to be good enough. Rest in knowing that God did the work. All we have to do is believe in him to secure your salvation.

The disciples then asked what miraculous signs they will see in order to believe. They refer back to their fathers who were shown miracles when manna was supplied in the desert. So, because of this they were expecting to have a miracle to show or prove that God is with them.

Has there been a time when you wanted "a sign" to validate God in your life?

Is this the right attitude to have? Why or why not?

And though, they received manna, or bread, in the desert, Jesus tells them that it is God that has given them true bread, bread from heaven. Verse 33, shows Jesus as the Bread of Life. It says,

"For the bread of God is he who comes down from heaven and gives life to the world."

Once the disciples realize that Jesus is the Bread of Life, they ask him to always give them this bread.

Do you ask Jesus for more of him?

How can you know Jesus more intimately, on a deeper level?

Day 3 – Read John 6:35-38 NIV

In these verses, we have an incredible promise from the Lord. Jesus declares that he is the bread of life. He compares our physical hunger and thirst with that of our spiritual hunger and thirst. In verse 35 (NIV) Jesus says,

> "I am the bread of Life. He who comes to me will never go hungry,
> and he who believes in me will never be thirsty."

Bread is the most basic of foods. Very few ingredients and yet, life giving. Water is the most important element for life. Our bodies are mostly water. This earth is mostly water. Bread and water are sustaining. Jesus says he is the Bread of Life. He is the One who sustains us. There are millions of people in the world that are hungry and thirsty, physically. They don't have enough food or clean water from day to day. And while that is really important and we should be making strides to help, there are also great numbers of people hungry and thirsty spiritually. Jesus promises that all who come to him will be accepted. He says,

> "…whoever comes to me I will never drive away."

He knows this is the Father's will. He knows that is why he came to earth and died on the cross. So that whoever comes to him does not have to hunger or thirst again. He will fulfill them, sustain them for eternity.

Look up some definitions of "drive away." Write a few here:

Write down some encouraging sentences to show God's promises using the definitions you found for "drive away." For example: "God will never chase me away." Or "God will never displace his love for me."

How can we relate this passage to tough times? How can this passage encourage us during trials?

What lesson can we learn from Jesus about obedience in this passage?

Day 4 – Read John 6:39-40 NIV

God's desire is that all would come to know him. In verse 39 Jesus says it is God's will that he will not lose anyone who God has given him. In other words, when someone has put their faith and trust in the Lord Jesus Christ, there is no losing your salvation. You can't all of a sudden stop God from loving you. Once you are his, you are sealed. You are God's and he is yours. In difficult times we need to hold onto to these promises. We need to recognize that no matter we go through we are his. Like a previous lesson discussed, nothing can separate us from his love.

The lesson is this….Jesus is the Bread of Life. He is the one that sustains us, in good times and in bad times. He is the constant one, the faithful one. He is our champion. He fights for us. Hang on to him, cling to him. Whatever comes your way, bring it to the Jesus who is our advocate. He will advocate for you, he will fight for you. Keep your eyes on him.

What's the greatest lesson you take from the verses in this passage?

What does the lesson, that you take away most, mean to you?

How does it change your attitude realizing God's promises to you?

Day 5 – Read John 6:25-40 NIV

After re-reading the entire passage for this week's lesson answer and reflect on the following questions:

What is it we must do?

Why is it so hard for some to accept that all they have to do is believe on the Lord Jesus Christ?

What have you learned about the seal?

Who *gives us* the true Bread of Life (trick question, read it carefully)?

Who *is* the Bread of Life? Write in it **BIG, BOLD, CAPITAL** letters!

This week's extra Tid-Bits:

Listen to "Come Thou Fount of Every Blessing"

This Week's Prayers:

_____
_____
_____
_____
_____
_____
_____
_____
_____
_____
_____
_____
_____
_____
_____
_____
_____
_____

This Week's Praises and Thanksgiving:

_____
_____
_____
_____
_____
_____
_____
_____
_____
_____
_____
_____
_____
_____
_____
_____
_____

Closing Remarks

Congratulations! You've completed this study. Throughout your time looking at some key truths of God's word, you have spent the last fifteen weeks learning things you may have already known or may have been new. No matter how you came into this study nearly four months ago I pray your faith has increased, your knowledge of the Lord has increased, and you have been refreshed by the Lord through growth in him.

There is one last tid-bit, however. It is not a "lesson" in the sense that the last fifteen weeks were laid out but it is a topic I want to take a few minutes to discuss with you. No matter what you do about your faith, how you live it, where you are with the Lord, one thing that seems to rapidly be going by the wayside is prayer. Our culture seems to be underestimating the power of prayer. So, in this last bit I want to give you five reasons we should be praying daily, all the time, really. Praying is not always formal; sitting in church with the pastor leading a long prayer. Your prayer life should never escape you. It can be just short bits of talking to God throughout your day. That's what prayer is, after all- talking to God. All too often our prayers can be conditional. We pray depending on our circumstances and if we feel like it. Prayer should not be based on just our feelings. We pray because it's a response to what God said to do and it builds us up. When we're in constant communication with God we are less likely to falter, follow the wrong path, or stray from his plan because we are hearing his voice. When prayer doesn't happen often we don't hear anything. The five reasons I've listed are just some of the reasons we are to pray. There are many more but read through these with careful consideration and reflection about your own prayer life. Never forget the importance and power of prayer!

Five Reasons to Pray

Part of our Obedience

We need to pray because God said so. 1 Thessalonians 5:17 (NIV) tells us to pray continuously. Most translations use the phrase,

"…without ceasing."

To cease, means to stop. So, we are to pray without stopping. Ephesians 6:18 (NIV) tells us to pray all the time, on every occasion. We are to pray about everything not just when we need something from the Lord. We are to pray when we need him to intercede for us, but also when we are thankful and rejoicing.

For the Sake of Love

We need to pray because of love. We pray because we love the Lord. When you have a best friend or a spouse, you don't go long without talking. And if you do, you know it is unusual. So, you'd make it appoint to talk to them quickly. How much more should we love the Lord? If it's been too long since you've prayed do you consider it unusual? Does it feel as though something is wrong? It should. We should feel a little off when we're not praying. If this is the case for you, begin today to talk to your Father. He's waiting.

Jesus is Our Example

We need to pray because Jesus prayed. In Mark 1:35, we see Jesus going off on his own to pray. Jesus is our example. In all that we do if we want to grow in Him, we strive to become more like him in character and attitude each day. Jesus knew the importance of praying, we need to follow his lead on this. Take time out every day to pray. By the way, praying in a quiet setting, maybe with some Bible verses being read is a great way to spend time with the Lord, but don't forget praying can happen continuously throughout your day. It can just be quick little prayers in your head here and there. As if you're just talking to him. The important thing is that you are communicating. Take time to talk to him and listen to him.

God Speaks Through Prayer

We need to pray because it's one way he speaks to us. Not only is prayer you talking to God, but it is also sitting still before the Lord (you'll recall lesson ten). When we are still before the Lord with an attitude of prayer we hear from the Lord. It is also in these quiet times that we can learn more about him. He reveals himself to us through prayer. Prayer creates a bond, a personal intimacy with the Father. It's just you and him time. It's a precious and special time.

We're Dependent

We need to pray because we are dependent on him. John 15:5 (NIV) says the Lord is the vine and we are the branches. Fruit on the vine cannot exist without the vine. It would die if it were apart from the vine. It's the same way with us. We cannot do anything apart from the Lord. We are dependent upon him. Because of this, we need to pray. We need to be continuously seeking him in order to grow in him and be sustained by him.

Keep your eyes on Jesus continuously and he will be faithful to complete his work in you (Philippians 1:6 NIV).